Skills4Peace

LEARN HOW TO DO PEACE !

FRAMEWORK &

USER MANUAL

BY

SHARON L ERNST

WALTER W SYLVESTER

ILLUSTRATIONS

BY

JEAN ROOSENBERG

About the Authors: Sharon L. Ernst and Walter W. Sylvester have been active in peacemaking for decades. In 2007 they were charter members of Mediators Beyond Borders International at its founding in Colorado.

Sharon Ernst is an executive and business consultant at sernst33134@yahoo.com. Walter Sylvester is a professional certified mediator and a licensed restorative peace skills practitioner/trainer with degrees in the Law and Mental Health Counseling at: waltersylvester@yahoo.com.

All interior illustrations are by Artist Jean Rosenberg, who specializes in book covers and illustrations. She can be contacted via email at: jiniroos2@msn.com.

Copyright 2019 by Sharon L. Ernst & Walter W. Sylvester
All rights reserved. No part of this book may be reproduced in any form whatsoever, by photography or copying or by any other means including by broadcast or transmission, by translation into any kind of language, nor by recording electronically or otherwise, without permission in writing from the authors, except by a reviewer, who may quote brief passages in reviews.

Published In the United States of America by WeDoPeace 5th Ed.

Dedication

This book is dedicated to all the Peace Builders, Peacemakers, Peace Doers and Peace Workers past, present and future tirelessly toiling in the vineyards of peace.

CONTENTS

7	Prologue Preface & Introduction
21	Chapter 1 - Formative Peace Skills
23	Mindfulness
31	Social & Emotional Learning
37	Chapter 2 - Connective Peace Skills
39	Face-to-Face Civil Conversations
45	Talking-Peace Circle in 80% Social Mode
63	Workplace Conferencing - Teamwork
71	Civic Smarts – A Citizen's Skillset
83	Chapter 3 - Responsive Peace Skills
86	Negotiation & Conflict Resolution
111	Mediation & Arbitration
137	Chapter 4 - Restorative Peace Skills
143	Affective or "I" Statements
144	Affective or Restorative Questions
146	Short & Quick Restorative Chats
147	Talking-Piece Circle in 20% Restorative Mode
149	Restorative Justice Circles
169	Restorative Conferences
177	Family Group Conferences
189	Chapter 5 – Curative Peace Skills
207	Epilogue
215	References & Resource
223	Graphics
241	Appendix – The US Constitution

PROLOGUE

"You have noticed that everything an Indian does is in a circle, and that is because the power of the World always works in circles, and everything tries to be round. In the old days when we were a strong and happy people, all our power came to us from the sacred hoop of the nation, and so long as the hoop was unbroken, the people flourished. The flowering tree was the living center of the hoop, and the circle of the four quarters nourished it. The east gave peace and light, and the south gave warmth, the west gave rain, and the north with its cold and mighty wind gave strength and endurance. This knowledge comes to us from the outer world with our religion. Everything the Power of the World does is in a circle. The sky is round, and I have heard that the earth is round like a ball, and so are all the stars. The wind, in its greatest power, whirls. Birds make their nests in circles, for theirs is the same religion as ours. The sun comes forth and goes down again in a circle. The moon does the same, and both are round. Even the seasons form a great circle in their changing, and always come back again to where they were. The life of a man is a circle from childhood to childhood, and so it is in everything where power moves. Our tepees were round like the nests of birds, and these were always set in a circle, the nation's hoop, a nest of many nests, where the Great Spirit meant for us to hatch our children."

Black Elk (1863-1950) Black Elk Speaks, John Neihar

PREFACE

The Skills4Peace Framework

Skills4Peace is a framework of peace skills we have created to provide the reader with a skillset that you can use to prevent a conflict before it starts or to resolve an existing conflict. We have identified the skills that have proven successful in various modalities of peacemaking/peacebuilding and assigned them to the five categories that form our Skills4Peace Framework:

FORMATIVE= 1) Mindfulness 2) Social & Emotional Learning
CONNECTIVE 1) Civility 2) Circles 3) Workplace 4) Civic Smarts
RESPONSIVE = 1) Negotiation 2) Mediation.
RESTORATIVE = 1) Restorative Justice & Practices.
CURATIVE = 1) Healing 2) Holistic 3) TIC 4) Anti-Violence

The Skills4Peace Framework is straightforward, sensible, and easy to comprehend. Everyone can see how the peace skills that fit into each category are interrelated; and how the categories, while independent of each other form a cohesive trajectory of skills that mirrors our own human development. Skills4Peace provides everyone the integrated societal skillset needed to successfully negotiate one's education – Pre-K thru college; one's career path – apprenticeship thru retirement; and community commitment – school team player thru informed citizen active in local civic affairs.

Skills4Peace is easily teachable and learnable whether as an integral component of the PreK-12 curriculum; as an independent study course either in person or online; or as providing the basis for facilitated dialogue to build trust, resolve conflict, and restore unity within the community. We hope over time that our Skills4Peace framework becomes mankind's go-to-skill set for the prevention/resolution of all its conflicts.

Sharon L. Ernst
Walter W. Sylvester

Skills4Peace Framework Chart

I FORMATIVE PEACE SKILLS:

A) Mindfulness: is being intensely aware of what you're sensing and feeling moment to moment without judgment.

B) Social & Emotional Learning (SEL):
Five cognitive, affective & behavioral competencies which are: Self-Awareness, Self-Management, Social Awareness, Relationship Skills and Responsible Decision Making.

II CONNECTIVE PEACE SKILLS

A) Face-To-Face Civil Conversations combine Respectful Speaking & Active Listening by all the parties to a conversation.

B) Group Talking-Piece Circles are meetings in any venue whose participants all use a talking piece to express themselves, build trust, connections & in time a community. (80% of the time).

C) Workplace Teams creating successful collaborative projects using Workplace Conferencing to resolve any problems that may arise.

D) Civic Smarts is a citizen's four-part skill set comprised of Civic Education, Civic Skills, Civic Dispositions, and Action Civics.

III RESPONSIVE PEACE SKILLS:

A) Negotiation - Discussing something with another to reach agreement.
B) Conflict Resolution – Resolving conflict using WEDOPEACE.
C) Mediation - Both sides retain a neutral mediator to assist them.
D) Arbitration – Like litigation it uses a contested trial before a decider.

IV RESTORATIVE PEACE SKILLS:

A) Affective or "I" Statements	(Informal)
B) Affective or Restorative Questions	(Informal)
C) Short & Quick Restorative "Chats"	(Informal)
D) Restorative Meetings (20% of Talking-Piece Circles)	(Semi-formal)
E) Restorative Justice Circles	(Formal)
F) Restorative Conference	(Formal)
G) Family Group Conference	(Formal)

V CURATIVE PEACE SKILLS:

A) Medicine Wheel B) Healing Circles C) Holistic Circles D) Primary Care Circles E) Trauma Induced Care D) CURE – An Anti-Violence Program.

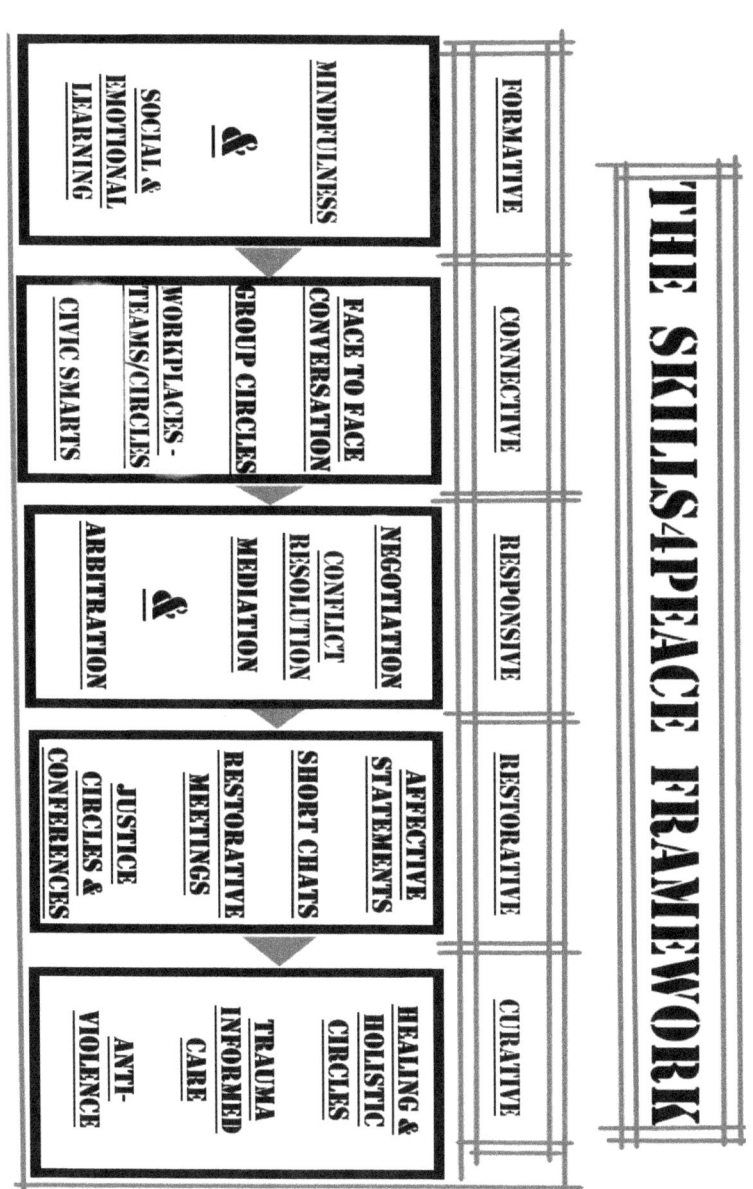

INTRODUCTION

Our modern-day societies replaced earlier Indigenous societies built upon a circular model. The obliteration of these circle-based societies resulted in the erosion of the connective fabric that created community and held them together - the inter-personal relationships existing between members. The loss of connectivity between members of today's top-down technological driven consumer societies is a global phenomenon.

It results in a universal lack of respect and empathy for one another as evidenced by the horrific amount of violence and mayhem members of our species inflict upon one another every day. So, when people seek ways to lessen the amount of violence in our societies, they need to find ways to reconnect us to each other to form communities much in the way weavers weave singular threads together to create whole new seamless fabrics.

To achieve this level of connectivity we believe the circular model of human community which builds, maintains, and repairs relationships needs to be reprised. We believe that this can be effectively done by all of us learning, mastering, and using in our daily lives the skillset of Formative, Connective, Responsive, Restorative & Curative Peace skills that form our Skills4Peace Framework as put forward in this manual.

All violence results from a failure to do peace. Conflict could be resolved without the use of violence if we all were taught and trained in our Skills4Peace just as we are all taught and trained in our ABC's. We conclude that the world can never be truly peaceful until its societies expend the time, effort and resources needed to teach and train everyone their Skills4Peace.

Learning how to do talking-piece circles provides a means for people to be able to connect with each other again. These circles are pro-actively used to build trust and a sense of community amongst their members eighty (80%) percent of the time when they meet to socialize; and leave the remaining 20% of their time available to meet in a restorative mode if needed to resolve problems that arise from time to time between members. They successfully resolve these occasional problems when they do arise because of the great amount of social capital they have built up over the 80% of the time that they meet socially; all this built-up good will is thus available to resolve the intra-group problems and disputes that inevitably arise.

The "Circle" movement is steadily growing since its beginnings in the 1970's in places like Canada and New Zealand. It got its start in these countries in response to dissatisfaction voiced by indigenous peoples of these countries who were increasingly unhappy over the treatment of their youth at the hands of those working in their countries existing juvenile justice and welfare systems.

They wanted to resurrect the restorative community-based justice system of their ancestors. This approach was based upon their conception of their community not as just a physical place, but as being comprised of the personal relationships that formed the connections between each other- connections which in turn tied them all together into a close-knit community much like the interwoven treads of a strong resilient fabric.

Their restorative circles form of justice was primarily interested in repairing the harm done to the victim and to the fabric of the community by the wrongdoer(s); with punishment of the wrongdoer being of secondary concern. They first wanted the wrongdoer(s) to take full responsibility for their part in doing the wrongful acts to the victims and the community before meeting in circle with the victims and members of the community at large. Wrongdoers would then reach agreement with everyone else in the circle as to the undertakings they needed to successfully complete to repair the harm done both to the victim(s) and to the community. Only after their fulfilling all those agreements of repair and restoration that they had made in open circle could offenders be welcomed back into the community and be accepted as full-fledged members once again.

The initial limited introduction of these restorative methods into the welfare system governing the indigenous segment of its population was so successful that New Zealand rolled out the circle process across its entire welfare system for all citizens under the name of

Family Group Conferences, which restorative practice has now spread to welfare systems in countries all around the globe under a variety of different names.

Two other advances in the development of Restorative Justice occurred In Canada - in Ontario, where the first Victim-Offender Mediation was done by probation officer Mark Yantzi in the 1970's; and in the Yukon Territory where a modernized version of the circle process with the participation of voluntary members of the local community was used by Judge Barry Stewart in his courtroom for sentencing in the 1990's. Since then, Restorative justice has made a slow, but steady advance into the legal systems of countries around the globe.

While first just used sparingly as a diversionary device in the juvenile courts, over the decades this circle-based restorative approach to wrongdoing has been increasingly adopted for not only dealing with non-violent crime but for violent crime as well; gradually being used at all stages of the prosecutorial continuum under the name of restorative justice.

After positive evidenced-based results in the legal field, with more than thirty-five states in the US now adopting legislation for using restorative justice both before and after prison in juvenile and adult courts, the restorative justice process was modified so it could be applied to societal problems beyond just those dealt with by the law enforcement and judicial systems. It is being now used so much more in the educational, social welfare arenas and other sectors of society than it is in the justice system that it has been renamed, when used in these non-legal areas, as either Restorative Practices, Restorative Approaches or Restorative Skills to reflect its newly gained acceptability and growing applicability.

So today the circle process is being used in all spheres and sectors of societies - in homes, daycare centers, schools, workplaces, courts, clubs, governmental agencies, and non-profits. Circles can transform groups, businesses, or organizations into connected, caring communities on all levels and across all divisions.

Some extremely passionate proponents contend that societies could be changed from violent ones into peaceful ones simply by everyone replacing the lecture style seating arrangements they now use with circular ones. While this may be a whimsical oversimplification and an exaggeration of the positive capabilities of restorative practices it does raise the question as to whether-or-not this restorative approach could be applied beyond a departmental level to a community-wide one; to challenge, if not replace, the hierarchal model upon which modern societies are built.

There are many towns and cities across the globe, including many within the United States, where the restorative approach has been adopted by a welfare department; or where a school or whole school district has adopted a student run restorative discipline program to replace a failed zero tolerance school discipline program based upon suspensions and expulsions, now infamously known as the "School to Prison Pipeline "- but there are none that are a match for those communities that have intentionally transformed their governmental agencies to the degree that they now call themselves "Restorative Cities" such as those emerging in the UK, Australia, Ireland and in other countries.

They may begin their transformation unnoticed by just applying the restorative approach to a few youth organizations or child welfare agencies that deal or engage with the disadvantaged children in their community. However, meeting with success in these limited applications, they quickly go beyond these initial tentative steps and intentionally take restorative practices to a whole new operational level across all sectors of their community by utilizing them in every aspect of communal life that deal with their children – in their homes, workplaces, schools, law enforcement agencies, courts, correctional institutions, and faith-based organizations.

In the UK the city of Kingston-on-Hull proudly holds the distinction of being the world's first restorative city; followed by the cities of Leeds and Bristol in the UK; Tallaght and Limerick in Ireland; Canberra and Newcastle in Australia; Como in Italy; and others across the EU. Indeed, in the United States, Detroit aspires to become the first restorative city. Lessons learned by these pioneering cities have accelerated the pace of other communities to embrace the goal of restructuring their existing hierarchal designed governmental services and social structures into circular restorative ones.

This emergence of restorative approaches to societal challenges beyond its initial application in the justice arena results from the failure of traditional western hierarchal structures to create communities that connect their residents within a framework of equality, connectivity, civility, and empathy – a framework that prevents violence from becoming the default skillset for resolving conflict at all levels of our societies.

All children can learn this framework as they progress through their PreK-12 school years. Our school-wide initiative we call "Skills4Peace" is represented metaphorically by the graphic of a moving train comprised of five box cars rolling down the track towards Peace - each boxcar carrying one of the five Skills4Peace categories as depicted on page 239.

Research now shows that teaching kids even some of these skills, such as those of social and emotional learning, dramatically improves classroom climate and leads to higher test scores, higher academic achievement, and higher graduation rates. In schools we call the restorative circles that are used by students as part of their on-campus self-disciplinary programs "Peer Circles" or "Justice Circles". These restorative justice circles replace the use of zero tolerance suspension and expulsion-based discipline programs.

CHAPTER 1

FORMATIVE PEACE SKILLS

A) Mindfulness

B) Social & Emotional Learning (SEL):

    1. Self-Awareness

    2. Self-Management

    3. Social Awareness

    4. Relationship Skills

    5. Responsible Decision Making

MINDFULNESS

ccBY-SA 30 Author: Radicalcourse http://radicalcourse.com

A. MINDFULNESS

What is Mindfulness?

Merrimack-Webster Dictionary:
"The practice of maintaining a nonjudgmental state of heightened or complete awareness of one's thoughts, emotions, or experiences on a moment-to-moment basis"

Jon Kabat-Zinn:
"Mindfulness means paying attention in a particular way: on purpose, in the present moment, and nonjudgmentally".

Thich Nhat Hanh:
" Mindfulness shows us what is happening in our bodies, our emotions, our minds, and in the world. Through mindfulness, we avoid harming ourselves and others".

Sylvia Boorstein:
"Mindfulness is the aware, balanced acceptance of the present experience. It isn't more complicated than that. It is opening to or receiving the present moment, pleasant or unpleasant, just as it is, without either clinging to it or rejecting it".

Mayo Clinic:
"Mindfulness is the act of being intensely aware of what you're sensing and feeling at every moment- without interpretation or judgment".

Psychology Today:
"Mindfulness is a state of active, open attention on the present".

Mindfulness began in 1979 when Dr. Jon Kabat -Zinn developed Mindfulness Based Stress Reduction (MBSR) at the UMass Medical School. By 2016 MBSR was in more than 200 medical centers, clinics and hospitals and is continuing to be adopted worldwide based upon a growing body of scientific studies showing that mindfulness interventions improve attention, self-control, and emotional resilience.

In the education arena teaching students mindfulness calming exercises such as breathing awareness have increased student ability to focus attention on tasks at hand; regulate and change how they react to their own thoughts, senses and emotions; and increase their development of empathy for what others may be going through which all contribute to an increased ability to adapt their established pattern of behavioral responses to deal effectively with changed circumstances.

One such breathing awareness exercise uses the acronym **STOP** to make to shift from a reactive and stressed mode to a mindfully responsive mode:

S - Stop. Whenever you notice stress or imbalance, pause and be aware of how you feel.

T - Take a breath. Simply bring your awareness into the breathing body, letting the sensations of the breath move into the forefront. Notice how your mind begins to settle a bit, bringing more clarity. Breath awareness harmonizes the cardiovascular systems in the body, while also calming the "alarm" centers in the more primitive parts of the brain, restoring full brain function. When we are stressed, we cannot think clearly or see any situation accurately.

O - Observe. Just notice how breathing begins to naturally bring balance to the systems of the body. Let this be felt. Also, look around. What is really happening, in the moment?

P - Proceed. Having shifted to a more mindfully responsive mode, take an action that is more skillful, appropriate, and best attuned to your situation.

Source: https://www.huffingtonpost.com/lisa-kring/the-5-main-tenets-of-mindful-parenting_b_4086080.html

Mindfulness is being embraced by all ages and all sectors of society as evidenced by the fact that while third graders in a Northern California elementary school classroom are being lead in the singing of a song written by beloved folksinger-songwriter Betsy Rose about Mindfulness (betsyrosemusic.org) far across the continent in South Florida law students are taking a course called Mindfulness In Law: Cultivating Tools for Effective Practice created and taught by Scott Rogers, the Founder & Director of the Mindfulness and Law Program at the University of Miami School of Law (www.miamimindfulnessinlaw.org). There are several mindfulness programs that have been developed for children and their teachers including MindUp and Mindful Schools (in the United States) and the Mindfulness in Schools Project (MISP) in the United Kingdom.

In some quarters in the child educational arena there has developed over the past decade a rivalry between some supporters of Mindfulness, which teaches students to slow down, focus moment to moment and build empathy and those who advocate the adoption of a longer established and many would say a much more scientifically proven childhood behavioral intervention program known as Social and Emotional Learning or SEL, which teaches students a set of skills such as how to mediate a dispute or be able to effectively communicate their emotions. SEL supporters point to research which shows SEL programs boost academic performance even as they socially and emotionally benefit children. Pennsylvania State psychologist Mark Greenberg co-authored a study, following hundreds of students from early childhood through young adulthood, finding poor social-emotional skills in kindergarten helped predict negative outcomes in the spheres of education, employment, criminal activity, substance use, and mental health. However, in many ways Mindfulness and SEL seen to complement each other- both seeking to teach children how to build self-awareness, effectively handle their emotions, and empathetically manage their relationships. Linda Lantieri, one of the founders of the SEL collaborative CASEL says the best approach to education combines Mindfulness and SEL skills rather than choosing one over the other. We agree with her conclusion and that is why we include both-of-them in Skills4Peace.

AN ONLINE COURSE:

The Palouse Mindfulness Course
(https://palousemindfulness.com)

VIDEOS FOR MINDFULNESS

PsychAlive (2013 January 23) What is Mindfulness with Jon Kabat-Zinn [Video File]. *YouTube.* Retrieved from https://www.youtube.com/watch?v=HmEo6RI4Wvs&feature=youtu.be

Happily (2015 December 7) Why Mindfulness Is A Superpower [Video File]. *YouTube.* Retrieved from https://youtu.be/w6T02g5hnT4

Smilecalm (2012 April 10) Take A Breath: Mindful Music for Children With Betsy Rose [Video File]. *YouTube.* Retrieved from https://www.youtube.com/watch?v=9iF7J2zlvtI&feature=youtu.be

Google (2007 November 12) Mindfulness with Jon Kabat-Zinn [Video File]. *YouTube.* Retrieved from https://youtu.be/3nwwKbM_vJc

TED 2013 January 11) All it takes is 10 mindful minutes | Andy Puddicombe [Video File]. *YouTube.* Retrieved from https://www.youtube.com/watch?v=qzR62JJCMBQ&feature=youtu.be

B. SOCIAL & EMOTIONAL LEARNING (SEL)

CASEL

Social and Emotional Learning can be traced all the way back to Greece and Plato, who in the Republic wrote, "By maintaining a sound system of education and upbringing, you produce citizens of good character". SEL became popular in 1995 by *NY Times* reporter Daniel Goleman's book entitled: <u>Emotional Intelligence: Why It Can Matter More Than IQ</u> which argued that character building skills can be taught.

Modern SEL began with work done by James Comer, a child psychologist, in the 1960's at Yale University in New Haven CT – The SEL movement was based there until 1996 when it was moved to The University of Illinois at Chicago under the name of The Collaborative for Academic, Social, and Emotional Learning) - CASEL.

"Social and emotional learning (SEL) involves the processes through which children and adults acquire and effectively apply the knowledge, attitudes, and skills necessary to understand and manage emotions, set, and achieve positive goals, feel, and show empathy for others, establish and maintain positive relationships, and make responsible decisions.

Effective SEL programming begins in preschool and continues through high school. CASEL (Collaborative for Academic, Social and Emotional Learning) has identified five interrelated sets of cognitive, affective, and behavioral competencies: The definitions of these five competency clusters for students are:

- **Self-Awareness:** The ability to accurately recognize one's emotions and thoughts and their influence on behavior. This includes accurately assessing one's strengths and limitations and possessing a well-grounded sense of confidence and optimism.

- **Self-Management:** The ability to regulate one's emotions, thoughts, and behaviors effectively in different situations. This includes managing stress, controlling impulses, motivating oneself, and setting and working to achieve personal and academic goals.

- **Social Awareness:** The ability to take the perspective of and empathize with others from diverse backgrounds and cultures, to understand social and ethical norms for behavior, and to recognize family, school, and community resources and supports.

- **Relationship Skills:** The ability to establish and maintain healthy and rewarding relationships with diverse individuals and groups includes communicating clearly, listening actively, cooperating, resisting inappropriate social pressure, negotiating conflict constructively, seeking & offering help when needed.

- **Responsible Decision Making:** The ability to make constructive and respectful choices about personal behavior & social interactions based on consideration of ethical standards, safety concerns, social norms, the realistic evaluation of consequences of various actions, and the well-being of self and others.

Effective Social and Emotional Learning programs.at: https://casel.org/guide/

VIDEOS OF SOCIAL AND EMOTIONAL LEARNING (SEL)

Edutopia (2013 May 27) 5 Keys to Social and Emotional Learning Success [Video File]. *YouTube.* Retrieved from https://www.youtube.com/watch?v=DqNn9qWoO1M&feature=youtu.be

CASEL (2017 August 28) SEL for Parents [Video File]. *YouTube.* Retrieved from https://www.youtube.com/watch?v=y2d0da6BZWA&feature=youtu.be

CASEL (2017 May 28) CASEL: Overview [Video File]. *YouTube.* Retrieved from https://youtu.be/Do1R67EkONI

AN ONLINE COURSE:

A certificate in SEL is offered by the **College of Saint Elizabeth** in partnership with **Rutgers University.**
http://sel.cse.edu/apply/

REVIEW QUIZ FOR CHAPTER ONE

1) John Kabat-Zinn's definition of Mindfulness is Mindfulness means paying attention in a particular way: on purpose, in the present moment, and _____.
a) place b) non-judgmentally c) without preconditions

2) MBSR stands for Mind Based _____ Reduction.
a) stress b) shame c) sleep

3) The breathing exercise called STOP allows you to shift form a responsive and stressed mode to a mindfully reactive mode.
(T OR F)

4) Mindfulness teaches students to slow down, focus moment to moment and build _____.
a) character b) empathy c) concentration

5) Mindfulness and Social & Emotional Learning _____ each other.
a) duplicate b) complement c) contradict

6) SEL was developed in Chicago and later moved to Yale in New Haven, CT. (T OR F)

7) SEL was referred to as Emotional Intelligence in the title of Daniel Goldman's book. (T OR F)

8) SEL now begins in Pre-K. (T OR F)

9) SEL develops 5 Competencies: Self & Social Awareness, Relationship Skills, and Self-Management – Name the fifth one.

10) CASEL stands for the Collaborative for _____, Social, and Emotional Learning.
a) American b) Accredited c) Academic

ANSWERS TO REVIEW QUIZ

1) b - nonjudgmentally

2) a – stress

3) F (shift form a reactive and stressed mode to a mindfully responsive mode

4) b- empathy

5) b- complement

6) F (developed at Yale and later moved to Chicago-CASEL)

7) T *Emotional Intelligence: Why It Can Matter More Than IQ*

8) T

9) The 5th competency is Responsible Decision Making

10) c- Academic

CHAPTER 2

CONNECTIVE

PEACE SKILLS

A) Face-to-Face Civil Conversations

B) Group - Talking-Piece Circles

C) Workplace Conferencing

D) "Civic Smarts"- A Citizen's Skillset

A) FACE-TO-FACE CIVIL CONVERSATION

Civil: relating to ordinary citizens and their concerns; courteous, polite —Merriam Webster

1) WHAT EXACTLY IS A CIVIL CONVERSATION?

At its simplest, a civil conversation is a dialogue between two people or a group that intends to build a better understanding. Participants don't have to agree—what matters is the act of listening to other people and learning their perspective. In that way, a civil conversation focuses on process rather than results. That means the conversation won't necessarily reach a pat resolution or an answer. The point is to raise important questions and (hopefully) hear one another's point of view.[1]

2) ABA RULES FOR ENSURING A CIVIL CONVERSATION

To ensure a civil conversation:

1. One of the hallmarks of a democracy is its citizens' willingness to express, defend, and perhaps reexamine their own opinions,
2. Show respect for the views expressed by others, even if you strongly disagree.
3. Be brief in your comments so that all who wish to speak have a chance to express their views.

4. Don't let disagreements or conflicting views become personal. Name-calling and shouting are not acceptable ways of conversing with others.
5. Let others express their views without interruption.

Remember that a frank exchange of views can be fruitful, so long as you observe the rules of civil conversation.[2]

3) SPEAKING SKILLS – SPEAKING CIVILLY WITH RESPECT

Always act in a polite manner using a respectful tone of voice.

Develop and use positive, non-threatening vocabulary.

Civil conversation takes place between two people who alternate their roles as sender and receiver of the information comprising their conversation.

Speech accounts for 30% of all civil conversation with 70% being non-verbal.

Non-verbal communication includes body language, eye contact, facial expressions and tone of voice.

Be mindful of your body language & avoid encroaching into the other's personal space.

Pause periodically to allow space for responses to your statements.

4) LISTENING SKILLS - ACTIVE LISTENING

How actively both speakers listen determines the effectiveness of their face-to-face conversation.

Give the speaker your undivided attention to show that you are listening.

Use body language and gestures to show that you are engaged.

Provide feedback.

Defer judgement.

Acknowledge the message.

Respond appropriately.

Drs Carl Rogers and Richard Farson rhetorically asked, "Just what does active listening entail, then? Basically, it requires that we get inside the speaker, that we grasp, from his point of view, just what it is he is communicating to us. More than that, we must convey to the speaker that we are seeing things from his point of view . . .".[3]

5) NONVIOLENT COMMUNICATION (NVC)

Another key proponent of the importance of how people speak and listen to each other was Dr. Marshall B. Rosenberg (PhD), who founded and developed what he called Nonviolent Communication. He conceived, developed, and promoted tirelessly Nonviolent Communication a/k/a Compassionate

Communication through decades of lecturing, teaching, and training NVC adherents all over the world.

Rosenberg and co-author Deepak Chopra, in their book *Nonviolent Communication: A language of Life 3rd Ed.*, ask the rhetorical question: "What is nonviolent communication? If "violent" means acting in ways that result in hurt or harm, then much of how we communicate—judging others, bullying, having racial bias, blaming, finger pointing, discriminating, speaking without listening, criticizing others or ourselves, name-calling, reacting when angry, using political rhetoric, being defensive or judging who's "good/bad" or what's "right/wrong" with people—could indeed be called "violent communication".[4] Rosenberg observed, "We can make life miserable or wonderful for ourselves and others depending upon how we think and communicate."[5]

The NVC process is a reframing process that guides us to reframe how we express ourselves, hear others and how we can resolve conflicts using a four-step model of observing without judging, express feelings, express and clarify your needs and express specific requests based upon your feelings and needs. It is based upon this fundamental principle – *Underlying all human actions are needs that people are seeking to meet; and understanding and acknowledging these needs can create a shared basis for connection, cooperation and more globally-peace.*[6]

FOOTNOTES:

A. FACE-TO-FACE CIVIL CONVERSATION

1. https://www.ncfp.org/2019/11/22/its-cool-to-be-kind-how-to-have-civil-conversations-in-todays-world/
2. https://www.americanbar.org/content/dam/aba/administrative/american_jury/groundrules.pdf,
3. Rogers, Carl and Farson, Richard. *Excerpt from 1957 article, Chicago (University of Chicago Industrial Relations Center) (25 pp.); also, in: Newman, R. G. / Danziger, M. A. / Cohen, M. (eds.), Communication in Business Today, Washington C.C. (Heath and Company) 1987*
4. Rosenberg, Marshall, and Deepak Chopra. Nonviolent Communication: A Language of Life, 3rd Edition: Life-Changing Tools for Healthy Relationships. 3rd ed. Encinitas, CA: PuddleDancer Pr. 3rd ed. Encinitas, CA: PuddleDancer Press, 2015.
5. Kashtan, Inbal and Kashtan, Miki at BayNVC at baynvc.org
6. https://www.nonviolentcommunication.com/

B) GROUP - TALKING-PIECE CIRCLES
The 80/20 Rule

Members of Talking-Piece Circles, such as Family, Neighbors, Workplace, and Community Public Circles, meet regularly to allow members to connect with each other and proactively build a strong bond of trust which is about 80% of the time. This bond in turn makes it easier for them to solve problems that arise amongst themselves the other 20% of the time – these disputes are handled in Restorative Mode Meetings (Page 142).

These talking-piece circles, also known as peace circles, are used to build trust or social capital building, problem solving, decision making, as well as brainstorming for like-minded circle participants who may be family, neighbors, club members or at times even various factions with opposing views, interests or positions that gather to air their differences - such as local police and community members of certain ethnic or age groups that believe that they are being profiled and/or brutalized; different racial, cultural or religious groups embroiled in confrontational matters; opposing political partisans or those on opposite sides of emotional issues who cannot otherwise seem to conduct civil discussions about their differences.

The Anatomy of a Circle

WeDoPeace Circles
"So We Can All Get Along"

1 The Physical Elements of The Circle

The physical set-up for a circle is simple in that it only consists of chairs arranged in a circle without any tables, desks, or other furniture within the circle so that everyone has an unobstructed view of everyone else sitting in the circle. In the middle of the circle of chairs on the floor there is usually placed what is called a "centerpiece" which consists of a rectangular piece of fabric with a number of items on it which have symbolic value to the participants of the circle and/or those charged with organizing it who are the "Circle Keepers".

We suggest that you always leave one seat in the circle open and available for any additional guest such as an invited speaker. Also, if there are more people than a basic circle can accommodate it can be used for forming a second circle around the first in a configuration called the "Fishbowl or Witness Circle". Fishbowls are often used to help a participant who seeks help from the circle regarding a problem he or she may be having with someone in the circle itself, or at their work or in their personal life. Those sitting outside can listen to those in the inner circle and if they have a suggestion to share with the group, they can do so by going to the empty seat in the inner circle to state their remarks and then return to their place in the outer circle again. This and other circle configurations such as the Popcorn, Spiral, Feedback and Wheelhouse Circles allow circle keepers to create circles best suited to achieve their objectives.[1]

A "Talking Piece" is an item which is in addition to those on the centerpiece and can be a stick, feather, rubber ball, stone, or whatever object the circle keepers and/or the circle participants choose to use to regulate the flow of speech during the circle. Whoever is holding the talking piece is the only one in the circle who has the right to speak. All the others in the circle must listen to the speaker attentively and wait to talk until it is their turn to hold the talking piece which is passed from one participant to the next usually in a clockwise direction.

A basic circle agenda in the classroom is: the creation of the ground rules and agreements by the whole class, choosing a talking piece, doing an opening ceremony, a check-in round followed by circle go-round of low risks prompts such as "where do you like to go on holiday ?" designed to help students learn about each other and as a warm-up for riskier prompts about possible classroom or campus issues, followed by discussion of a previously agreed upon topic or comments on an academic topic or assignment, then a check-out round followed by a closing ceremony. As students in a reoccurring circle become better acquainted with the "getting to know you" prompts, these prompts will be replaced with more status type check-ins updating each other on their current feelings and activities.

School staff can also use this basic circle agenda for building community, dealing with administrative differences, brainstorming and problem solving.

2. The Guidelines of a Circle

Peace Circle participants abide by a handful of basic guidelines allowing for a smoothly functioning circle:

1. Respect The Talking Piece (Give the Piece Holder Your Full Attention, Handle the Piece with Care,

Give Full Attention to Your Truth When You Hold It & Speak To The Center of The Circle)
2. Speak from the Heart
3. Listen From the Heart
4. Speaking Spontaneously (No Need to Rehearse What You Will Say While Awaiting Your Turn)
5. Speaking Economically (Don't Speak Too Long)

3. Circle Specific Agreements

While the guidelines listed above apply to all circles there can be additional agreements that are circle specific for conducting a circle which are made by the participants of each circle by consensus using a method such as **Fist to Five,** also called fist of five, to poll team members and help achieve consensus. Fist to Five is like Thumbs Up, Thumbs Down or Thumbs Sideways. These circle specific agreements can be for such things as keeping confidentiality; using a second circle keeper called a Guardian to assist the first by watching the energy, timing and needs of the circle; deciding to rotate the role of the circle keeper among members for each new meeting of an ongoing circle; actively staying in the circle until all issues are resolved; not using obscene language or using only one particular talking piece in all meetings of that circle group. If a proposed agreement cannot be agreed to by consensus it is not adopted. An ongoing circle will periodically reconsider their agreements to make sure that they still suit their purpose as their circle evolves over time.

4. Circle Keepers

The role of the Circle Keeper, who is also a participant in the Talking Piece Circle (which is in marked contrast to the role of a mediator who is never a party in a mediation) is to politely enforce the guidelines and any circle specific agreements while promoting and maintaining an atmosphere of respect, safety, and optimism in the circle. Circle Keepers also summarize the successes of the circle as it progresses. They also clarify what issues are yet to be resolved by the circle participants.

Circle Keepers ask rounds of questions. Once the circle has commenced, they always ask a check-in round to allow everyone a chance to place their voices in the circle which insures everyone is truly present in mind as well as body. If the circle is a newly formed circle, then in addition to saying their names each person may give a brief self-introduction; whereas in an ongoing circle the check-in may be used by members to briefly update others about their activities or express their hopes for what the meeting will be able to accomplish. The check-in round begins with a volunteer who after speaking passes the talking piece clockwise. Members who are not ready to speak can pass it on without speaking; it being understood that they will be given another chance after the rest have completed their check-ins.

Succeeding rounds of questions are designed to facilitate the progression of the circle to attain the core intention for which it was created. If the intention is to build a sense of community (i.e., a Talking Piece Circle) then rounds of questions will be asked that tend to foster and deepen connections between the participants. If, on the other hand, the intention for the circle was to address a specific situation or issue (i.e., a Restorative Mode Meeting) then the rounds of questions that follow will consist of those designed to engender a restorative dialogue about that issue; the circle keeper(s) first making it clear to all what the issue is that is going to be addressed by the circle.

If the members of the circle, for whatever reasons, are not ready to have a restorative dialogue than the circle keeper(s) need to suspend the effort and not continue dealing with it at this circle. They can address it at a later circle if after doing more preparatory work with the participants, those participants decide that they want to finally deal with the matter in a new circle.

5. Stages of A Circle

The four general stages of the circle process are:

1. Mutual Acceptance that the process can work by both the parties involved and the community-as-a-whole.

2. Thorough Preparation – Separate preparatory circles are held by those with like interests to discuss concerns and be prepared to take part effectively in the main circle gathering.

3. Main Circle Gathering – The parties and all their supporting circles come together to express their needs and fears and to develop mutually acceptable solutions to the issues discussed.

4. Monitoring – Post-circle follow-ups are used to determine progress in fulfilling agreements made and for modifying terms of these agreements if the need to do so is dictated by changed conditions.

6. Outline for Doing Peace Circles

There are many outlines to guide Circle Keepers in creating and conducting the various kinds of circles covered in this book. They can all be modified by the circle keepers to fit the particular facts of the situation they are being asked to address and the goals being sought by those requesting a circle; assuming that the circle process is found suitable to be used in the first place. They are either used to make connections by building trust amongst their participants or restoratively by resolving a conflict between one or more of their participants in a way that restores their relationship to each other and to others in the circle.

7. A Generic Circle Outline

Pre - Circle Preparations

Circle Keepers Pre-Circle Preparations

Circle Keepers usually work in pairs dividing circle tasks between themselves, although they are trained to be able to keep a circle on their own and often do. The Circle Keepers meet individually with each person involved in the situation or concerned with the issue for which the circle is being formed to address. They will explain to each of them how the circle process works, and the role played by the talking piece, centerpiece, standard circle guidelines, additional circle specific agreements made by consensus, opening, and closing ceremonies and how and when each of these items will be chosen and employed.

Based upon the information they have gained by talking with each participant, the circle keepers will then design rounds of questions they will be asking the circle participants once the circle is convened beginning with rounds of introductory check-in questions, then rounds of relationship and trust building questions to develop a sense of group cohesiveness which will provide circle participants with a sense of safety sufficient to allow the Circle Keepers to ask the key questions they have designed to foster a dialogue within the circle that addresses the situation or key issue(s) for which the circle was formed to deal with in the first instance.

Preparing The Circle Venue

When the Circle keepers arrive at the venue, they, and their volunteer assistants:

1. Arrange chairs in a circle.
2. Create a center piece using items having symbolic significance for some, or all, the participants.
3. Set up a whiteboard on a tripod or bring blank newsprint to post about the room to write on.
4. Have volunteers greet participants as they enter the venue and encourage them all to socialize.
5. Everyone is seated in their chairs in a circle facing each other without any furniture between them except for the centerpiece which is on the floor.

The Circle Begins

1. Circle Keepers introduce themselves and begin the Circle with the agreed upon opening ceremony consisting of drumming, singing chanting praying or opening quotations performed by volunteers who usually do a similar type of closing ceremony as well.

2. Circle Keepers begin by explaining what tasks each of them will be doing during the circle with one acting as the Circle Keeper who asks the prompts (rounds of questions); and the other acting as the Guardian who keep an eye on the time and needs of the circle using a chime or rattle to intervene as needed. The Guardian also handles the housekeeping matters and announces to the circle's members the number of break times, their length, and the location of the rest room facilities.

3. The Circle Keeper will review the standard circle guidelines regarding the use of the talking peace, speaking and listening form the heart, speaking spontaneously and everyone speaking economically.

4. If it is a continuing circle, the Circle Keeper will have the participants review their ongoing agreements to find out whether they want to delete any of the old ones or add any new ones. If they want to make some changes suggestions are written on the whiteboard or on the newsprint for consideration and then a vote is taken by all the participants with only those new agreements that have been approved by consensus being adopted.

5. If it is a new first time circle the Circle Keeper will ask participants to suggest what agreements they want to have the circle vote upon. After writing them on a

whiteboard or on sheets of newsprint posted on the walls a vote of all the participants will be taken on each one using either the five to fists or thumbs up voting methods. Only those agreements that achieve a consensus vote of approval can be adopted.

6. A Check-in question asking members to introduce themselves is posed and answered first by the Circle Keeper who starts the round off by introducing him or herself then passing the talking piece clockwise so each of the other participants can introduce themselves in turn.

If the circle is a talking-piece circle that has not been convened to address a specific issue or conflict situation, then rounds of trust building questions will follow and continue until the circle is closed unless an activity has been planned. If there is an activity on the agenda such as a Guest Speaker or a topic for discussion it happens at this point in the circle with the Circle Keeper suspending the use of the talking piece during this activity portion of the circle.

A basic circle agenda for use in the classroom could be: the creation of the ground rules and agreements by the whole class, choosing a talking piece, doing an opening ceremony a check-in round followed by circle go-round of low risks prompts such as "where do you like to go on holiday ?" designed to help students learn about each other and as a warm-up for riskier prompts about possible classroom or campus issues, followed by discussion of a previously agreed upon topic or comments on an academic topic or assignment, then a check-out round followed by a closing ceremony. As students in a reoccurring circle become better acquainted those "getting to know you" type prompts will be replaced with more status type check-ins updating each other on their current feelings and activities. School staff can also use this basic circle agenda for building community, dealing with administrative differences, brainstorming and problem solving.

If, on the other hand, the circle has been called to deal with a situation or conflict issue that the participants want to address it becomes a restorative-type peace circle (a/k/a Restorative Mode Meeting), with the Circle Keepers deciding when it is appropriate to start asking key restorative type questions designed to engender a restorative dialogue.

If the participants avoid the issue than more and deeper questions may need to be asked. If the participants avoid answering these deeper questions, then the Circle Keepers should suspend the circle and meet participants privately; either on an individual basis, or in smaller circles comprised of those who share the same interests in the issue in-order-to reconsider their options.

7. Sometimes it may be advisable for the Circle Keeper or Guardian to suspend the use of the talking piece to allow informal conversation amongst participants to help bring the issue to the surface where it can be addressed by all. In the alternative, the facilitator that is acting as the Guardian may call for a time of silence so that participants can center themselves and consider the possible actions or decisions, they want to make such as whether to enter-into a restorative dialogue now or end the circle meeting and reconvene it at a future time.

8. Once the participants have a restorative dialogue about the situation or issue and reach by consensus vote an agreement as to what needs to be done to make things right, those agreements should be put into writing to avoid any misunderstandings. The agreement should include a monitoring method to follow up and check on whether the terms of the agreement are being upheld or not by all parties. There also needs to be a plan for coming back to circle to discuss any problems arising in the event the terms are not being met.

9. The Circle Keeper than starts a Check-out round of questions using the talking piece to end the circle.

10. A Formal Closing of the circle using an agreed upon closing ceremony consisting of drumming, singing chanting, praying or a closing quotation is performed by the same volunteers who did the opening ceremony.

Post-Circle Gathering

A social gathering after the circle is formally closed consists of a social time with refreshments. This social time is a key part of the circle's healing process and participants should be encouraged to stay and socialize.

FOOTNOTES

B. GROUP - TALKING-PIECE CIRCLES

1. Teaching Restorative Practices with Classroom Circles (Page 21) Amos Clifford, Center for Restorative Process Developed for San Francisco Unified School District: https://www.sfusd.edu/services

GENERIC TRUSTBUILDING OR CONNECTION BUILDING TALKING PIECE CIRCLE OUTLINE

START THE CIRCLE
1- Circle Keeper & Guardian Arrive
2- Announce Purpose of Circle is to build trust.
3- Open All Circles with An Opening Ceremony
Drumming, Singing Chanting Praying or Quotations.
4- Review the Standard Guidelines for All Circles
5- Create or Update Agreements Of This Specific Circle

DO THE CIRCLE
6- Check-In Round Question Using the Talking Piece
i.e.: *What is your name and how to you feel?*
7- Do Several Community or Trust building Round(s)
i.e.: *What do people like about you best?*
(See More Questions from U of Maryland Law School)5
8- Activity - Guest Speaker or Topic of Interest
9 - Check-Out Round Question for All Circles
i.e.: *What is your takeaway from this circle?*

COMPLETE THE CIRCLE
10- Close All Circles with A Closing Ceremony
11- All Circles Host a Post Gathering for Refreshments

VIDEOS FOR CONNECTIVE TALKING-PIECE CIRCLES

Restorative Justice Council (2015 April 16) Moving On [Video File]. *YouTube*. Retrieved from https://youtu.be/fWtFtWY3Hh8

Restorative Resource (2015 April 28) The Animated Intro to Restorative Justice [Video File]. *YouTube*. Retrieved from https://youtu.be/rE7rPahe38I

StMattsTosa(2015 January 29) Restorative Practices/ Circle Keeping [Video File]. *YouTube*. Retrieved from https://youtu.be/5FUItXPUEpU

RestorativeCircles(2009) Dominic Barter On Restorative Justice [Video File]. *YouTube*. Retrieved from https://youtu.be/o-AUwX61-34

Edwin Rutsch (2012 September 20)+Jay Pranis & Edwin Rutsch: How To Build a Culture of Empathy with Circle Process [Video File]. *YouTube*. Retrieved from https://youtu.be/Mj8feRbZSAQ

Cassandra Beanland Talking Circle (2015 May 5) [Video File]. *YouTube*. Retrieved from https://youtu.be/Y-ttcmMK1mc

The Circle Way (2014 March 17) Components of The Circle Way: Part 1 [Video File]. *YouTube*. Retrieved from https://youtu.be/NU9IbT_IX8A

The Circle Way (2014 March 17) Components of The Circle Way: Part 2 [Video File]. *YouTube*. Retrieved from https://youtu.be/IfR1bHvoTvw

The Circle Way (2014 March 17) Components of The Circle Way: Part 3 [Video File]. *YouTube*. Retrieved from https://youtu.be/OChITc4pvoU

C) WORKPLACE CONFERENCING

WORKFORCE - BASED "TEAM CIRCLES"

Conflict in the workplace is a fact of life that causes extensive personnel, productivity, and economic losses. **Team Circles** are used as workplace-based conflict prevention (80% of the time) and conflict resolution (20% of the time) program akin to the Talking-Piece Circles and Restorative Circle Meetings we described earlier in non-workforce environments.

Thus, **Team Circles** can be used as either **Talking-Piece Circles** on a regular basis on all levels and sectors of an organization to proactively build team cohesiveness eighty (80%) percent of the time; or as **Workforce Meetings,** the other twenty (20%) percent of the time, to resolve isolated disruptive incidents between workforce team members; akin to the Restorative Meetings in non-workforce situations.

Alternatively, **Workplace Conferencing** can be used to deal effectively with more destructive behavior or widespread grievances that involve teams, numerous employees, or departments i.e., employee misconduct, bullying, over- aggressive management, sexual harassment, performance issues and discrimination.

ADVANTAGES OF WORKPLACE CONFERENCING

Workplace Conferencing is preferable to mediation and other ADR modalities that all have a narrow focus on a problem when serious wrongdoings and/or conflict strike across an organization and are not confined to just one department. In workplace conferencing the facilitators ask everyone involved what happened, how it affected each of them and what each of them thinks should be done to make things right and reunify the team.

The wrongdoer(s) having taken responsibility for their acts must agree to the terms reached by all the participants by consensus spelling out what they will need to do to repair the harm done and agree not to repeat their wrongful actions and not disrupt the team with other bad behavior again.

Some of the participants volunteer or are appointed to check in future months that the wrongdoers are complying with the terms of the Workplace Conference Agreement. Subsequent conferencing may be necessary if the terms are not complied with accompanied by the threat that continued non-compliance could send the matter upstairs for management and HR to resolve.

EEO HISTORY

Modern workplace practices and training developed from and because of the creation of the EEOC in Washington. The Equal Employment Opportunity Commission (EEOC) enforces EEO laws and provides oversight and coordination of all federal EEO regulations, practices, and policies. EEOC is an independent federal agency originally created by congress in 1964 to enforce Title VII of the Civil Rights Act of 1964.

Equal Employment Opportunity (EEO) is about ensuring that work environments are free from unlawful discrimination and harassment, and provides employees with equal opportunities for jobs, training, and development. It was during the 20th century that EEO evolved, and EEO laws and regulations were created. On September 24, 1965, President Lyndon Johnson issued Executive Order 11246. This Order stated that the head of each executive department and agency shall establish and maintain a positive program of equal employment opportunity for all civilian employees and applicants for employment within its jurisdiction.
This Executive order led to the first EEO Executive Order.

. https://www.ttb.gov/eeo/history.shtml

WeDoPeace Teams				
Domestic Violence	Joe	Kay	Ann	Pete
Business Disputes	Roger	Sally	Sol	Mike
Neighbors	Jamie	Bill	Tom	Sid
Work Places	Harry	Tina	Jim	Dan

"Jim, from our Workplace Peace Team, will be calling you back at 4:30 today to schedule a Peace Circle with your employees."

THE COST OF CONFLICT IN THE WORKPLACE

It's a fact of life that when people work together there's going to be conflict. It is also a fact that Conflict in the workplace is costly because as reported on page 3 of the May 2005 issue of the Washington Business Journal: "It causes lost productivity leading to absenteeism, customer loss, sabotage, increased bullying, toxic relationships, lost sales, lost income, lost wages and lost profits with managers spending 25-40% of their time dealing with conflict"

According to a 2010 posting at www.entrepeneur.com all U.S. employees in 2008 spent 2.8 hours per week dealing with conflict. This amounts to $359 billion in paid hours (based on average hourly earnings of $17.95) and the equivalent of 385 million working days (nationwide).[1]

Some triggers that can cause conflict are organizational changes, miscommunication, scarcity of resources, prejudices, values incongruence, personality clashes, workloads, and stress.

The total value of lost work time due to elevated stress levels caused by unresolved conflict is estimated to be over $1.5 billion annually[2] not to mention the cost of increasing numbers of employees suffering from mental health problems seeking help from professional mental health providers.[3]

A Consulting Psychologists Press (CPP) study found the primary causes of workplace conflict relate to personality clashes, followed by stress and workload.[4]

VIOLENCE IN THE WORKPLACE

The foregoing costs do not include the toll on human life when the conflict escalates into violence - according to the US Bureau of Labor Statistics two million Americans report being victims of workplace violence every year. In 2014, of the 4,821 workplace deaths, 409 of them were the results of workplace attacks.

OSHA places workplace violence into four major types of categories: criminal intent, customer/client, personal relationship, and worker-on-worker strained relations with the later causing 60- 80 % of all difficulties that arise in the workplace.[5]

Workers need to be observant of certain common behaviors on the part of a co-worker that can be indicative of future violence by them such as:

- Verbal threats to others
- Paranoia
- Changes in behavior, i.e., mood swings
- Decline in job performance
- Violation of company rules
- Increased use of alcohol or drugs

- Unexplained absenteeism
- Depression and/or withdrawal
- Suicidal remarks
- Resisting changes at work
- Persistent complaining of unfair treatment.
- Emotional outbursts to criticism

COSTS TO REPLACE DEPARTING EMPLOYEES

Workplace conflict is a decisive factor in more than 50% of all employee departures.[6]

Ernst & Young reports that the cost of losing and replacing an employee may be as high as 150% of the departing employee's annual salary.[7]

COST OF LITIGATION

In addition to losses arising out of lost production and cost of employee replacement there is the cost to business from litigation arising from conflicts on the job.

More than 50% of employers report being sued by an employee.[8]

The national average compensatory award in employment practice liability cases rose from $133,691 in 1997 to $250,000 in 2003.[9]

Unresolved workplace conflict issues can end up in litigation that can cost a company from $50,000 to $100,000 in attorney fees and 3 to 5 years to settle.[10]

REASONS FOR CONFLICT IN BUSINESSES

Differing Values: Conflict arises when workers do not respect, agree with, or accept each other's values.

Miscommunicating: Different ways of communicating can cause disputes arising out of employees not fully understanding one another and/or their managers.

Incongruent Interests: Non-aligned goals that place the personal goals of the employee at odds with those of the employer can cause ongoing conflict.

Scarce Resources: Competition for scarce resources causes conflict between workers.

Personality Problems: Conflicts can arise in a business like in any other kind of workplace when there is a personality problem between two team members.

Slacking Off: Habitual slackers arouse anger in their co-workers resulting in an ongoing conflict.

VIDEOS FOR CHAPTER FOUR - WORKPLACE TEAM CIRCLES

IIRP Graduate School (2014 November 14) The Challenge of Building a Restorative Youth Services Organization [Video File}. *YouTube.* Retrieved from https://youtu.be/jnuOwZT-Jeg

Zehr Institute for Restorative Justice (2016 December 12) Restorative Justice and the Practice of Law [Video File} YouTube. Retrieved from https://youtu.be/71esnfvJnz0

TEDx Talks (2016 April 1)) Embedding Restorative Practices in Community | Paul Chambers | TEDxStPeterPort [Video File] *YouTube.* Retrieved from https://youtu.be/ebGlV0jQcek

ADR International Group Inc. (2013 November 11) Restorative Justice Overview and Application to the Workplace [Video File]. *YouTube.* Retrieved from https://youtu.be/XOysVPmr-Js

The Circle Way (2014 September 30) Circle at the Core of Business Practice [Video File]. YouTube. Retrieved from https://youtu.be/KcVh1PHstEs

The Circle Way (2014 October 15) Circle in Healthcare Leadership [Video File]. YouTube. Retrieved from https://youtu.be/wSajfeOm7sg

The Circle Way (2014 September 30) The Circle Way – International [Video File]. YouTube. Retrieved from https://youtu.be/iEj-zfY5ndM

FOOTNOTES

C. WORKPLACE TEAMS

1. National Academy of Program Administrators, freedictionary.com.
2. Benchmarking Diversity: A First Look at New York City Foundations and Nonprofits, Foundation Center, 2009.
3. Lawler, Jennifer (June 10, 2010): The Real Cost of Workplace Conflict, www.entrepreneur.com.)
4. Johnston, Erin, MSW, LCSW: Workplace Conflict is Expensive (July 5, 2011), CFR Mediation Blog.)
5. Warren Shepel: Workplace Trends Linked to Mental Health Crisis in Canada, 2002.)
6. Workplace Conflict and How Business Can Harness it to Thrive, CPP Global Human Capital Report
7. Managing Differences: How to Build Better Relationships at Work and Home, 4th edition; Kreisman,
8. Johnston, Erin, MSW, LCSW: Workplace Conflict is Expensive (July 5, 2011), CFR Mediation Blog.)
9. www.dhrm.virginia.gov/resources/conference presentations/anoverviewofEmployeeDispute Resolution conflict)
10. Society for Human Resource Management survey cited in the USA Today article, "Workers Win More Lawsuits, Awards" March 27, 2001.)
11. JuryVerdictResearch.com, LRP Publications (2004)
12. Taylor, Robin: Workplace Tiffs Boosting Demand for Mediators, National Post (March 17, 2020)

D) "CIVIC SMARTS"- A CITIZEN'S SKILLSET

In each of the three previous sections of this chapter we have gradually widened the use of our connective peace skills. First, using the skills of respectful speaking and active listening to foster civil face to face conversations; Second, employing talking-piece circles to build trust and a sense of community among group members; Third, by adopting DEI guidelines to create unified, cohesive, and productive workforces in the workplace.

What we call "Civic Smarts", is the Fourth and widest arena within which to utilize our connective peace skills. As its name implies, "Civic Smarts" is the skillset we must master to effectively take part in the civic life of our community, state, and nation.

Being an informed, thoughtful, and active citizen of a democracy, such as ours, requires a combination of three essential skills - civic knowledge, civic skills, and civic dispositions -This three-part skillset is what we call "Civic Smarts". Every citizen needs to master these three skills for a democracy such as the United States of America is to survive over the long term.

(Note: A copy of the US Constitution is in the Appendix of this book)

CIVIC KNOWLEDGE

Civics learning is the acquisition of knowledge, the intellectual skills, and the applied competencies that citizens need for informed and effective participation in civics and democratic life. [1]

CivXNow, a project of iCivics, a bipartisan coalition of academic and research institutions, and philanthropic organizations, has taken up the goal of iCivics founder, the late Supreme Court Justice Sandra Day O'Conner, to revitalize the mission of schools in fulfilling their vital role of being the source of quality civic learning for all. So, on its website, CivXNow answers the question "What is Civics?" as follows: "In its broadest sense, civics (also known as "civic education" or "civic learning") is the lifelong process that makes people into active, responsible, and knowledgeable members of their communities—which range from their schools and towns or neighborhoods to the whole nation and even the world. Civic learning occurs in families, in religious congregations and other associations, in political campaigns, and on news websites, among many other venues". [2]

CIVIC SKILLS

Citizens to be capable of fully engaging in civic and political life, must possess a minimum of civic skills. Civic skills include personal communication skills, knowledge of political systems, and the ability to critically think about civic and political life (Comber 2003).[3]

To be good citizens we must develop intellectual and participatory skills that include:

(i) communication skills (i.e., speaking, listening, vocabulary).

(ii) writing skills to express facts and opinions).

(iii) organizing skills (i.e., leadership and teaching.

(iv) social media skills in managing civic organizations).

(v) critical thinking skills (i.e., collecting information, evaluating information, drawing conclusions, and evaluating those conclusions).

(vi) rational thinking skills (i.e., the ability to consider the relevant variables of a situation and to be able to access, organize, and analyze relevant information to arrive at a sound conclusion informed by evidence).

(vii) collective decision-making skills (i.e., participating in democratic deliberation leading to collective decision-making).[4]

CIVIC DISPOSITIONS

We just mentioned the need for a citizen to have "the necessary disposition" to be able to use Civic Knowledge effectively. The third essential component of civic education, civic dispositions, refers to the traits of private and public character essential to the maintenance and improvement of constitutional democracy.

Traits of private character such as moral responsibility, self-discipline, and respect for the worth and human dignity of every individual are imperative. Traits of public character as public spiritedness, civility, respect for the rule of law, critical mindedness, and willingness to listen, negotiate, and compromise are also indispensable to democracy's success.5.

"Civic dispositions that contribute to the common good were identified in the *National Standards for Civics and Government*. Those dispositions or traits of private and public character can be summarized as:

1) Becoming an independent member of Society: Accepting responsibility for the consequences of one's actions and fulfilling the moral and legal obligations of membership in a democratic society.

2) Assuming the responsibilities citizenship:
Being informed about public issues, voting, paying taxes, serving on juries, performing public service, and serving in positions commensurate with one's talents.

3) Respecting individual worth and human dignity: Behaving in a civil manner, considering the rights and interests of fellow citizens, and adhering to the principle of majority rule with the right of the minority to dissent.

4) Engaging in civic affairs thoughtfully and effectively: being informed prior to voting; or engaging in civil and reflective discourse; or assuming a leadership position.

5) Promoting a healthy constitutional democracy: Being attentive to public affairs, learning about constitutional values and principles, and monitoring the adherence of political leaders to them.[6]

The importance of civic dispositions, or the "habits of the heart," as Alexis de Tocqueville called them are, in the long run, probably of more consequence than the civic knowledge or civic skills a citizen may command - Judge Learned Hand, in 1944 stated the vital role which civic dispositions play in the preservation of our liberty: *"Liberty lies in the hearts of men and women; when it dies there, no constitution, no law, no court can save it; no constitution, no law, no court can even do much to help it. While it lies there, it needs no constitution, no law, no court to save it"*.[7]

ACTION CIVICS

According to the Center of Civic Education, civic education is a means to actively engage people in the practice of democracy in the United States and other countries.[8] So, in addition to just teaching students the basics like what is in the U.S. Constitution[9] and how a bill becomes a law there is now a movement in our K-12 schools that pairs the teaching of these facts with the development of civic attitudes and behaviors.[10]

These programs aim to develop students' civic skills, knowledge, and dispositions to the point that permits them to participate in civic engagement as students. One such program is called Action Civics run by a non-profit Generation Citizen that teaches it to middle and high school students.

The courses give students opportunities for real-world engagement as they work to solve community problems. The course framework encourages students to think through an issue such as gang violence, homelessness, etc. by researching its root cause, developing an action plan, getting involved in their

community through engagement tactics and presenting their efforts to their class.

At the end of the 2016-17 school year, 90 percent of students self-reported that they believed they could make a difference in their community. With the goal of encouraging long-term civic engagement, Generation Citizen classes combine civics and service learning through a student-centered approach.11

A good example of such a program expanded on a state-wide scale is the one created when Massachusetts Gov. Charlie Baker signed Ch 296 of the Acts of 2018, entitled: *An Act to promote and enhance civic engagement.* This law includes provisions related to student-led civics projects:

"Every student regardless of race, class, ethnicity, religion, education, gender, gender identity, sexual orientation, or disability has the right to civics education, including effective pedagogy and applied learning.

Civics learning is the acquisition of knowledge, the intellectual skills, and the applied competencies that citizens need for informed and effective participation in civics and democratic life. A non-partisan, student-led civics project is based on action civics—a process of applying civic knowledge, skills, and dispositions to mobilize change leading to systems impact."

The law requires that each public school, serving students in the eighth grade and each public high school, "shall provide not less than 1 student-led, non-partisan civics project for each student. Civics projects may be individual, small group or class wide designed to promote citizen's ability to:

(i) analyze complex issues.
(ii) consider differing points of view.
(iii) reason, make logical arguments and support claims using valid evidence.
(iv) engage in civil discourse with those who hold opposing positions; and
(v) demonstrate an understanding of the connections between federal, state, and local policies, including issues that may impact the student's school or community".

In addition, the law authorizes:

"Promotion of youth membership on municipal boards, and a non-partisan high school voter challenge to encourage eligible students to register or pre-register to vote and participate in municipal and state elections."[12]

FOOTNOTES

D. CIVIC SMARTS

1. Branson, Margaret Stimmann. The Role of Civic Education A Forthcoming Education Policy Task Force Position Paper from the Communitarian Network (September 1998)
2. A Project of ICivics https://www.civxnow.org/what-is-civics.
3. Comber, Melissa K. "Civics Curriculum and Civic Skills: Recent Evidence." CIRCLE: The Center for Information & Research on Civic Learning and Engagement https://eric.ed.gov/?id=ED498908
4.-8. https://civiced.org/papers/articles_role.html
9. (https://www.pbs.org/newshour/classroom/app/uploads/2013/11/summary-of-the-US-Constitution.pdf)
10. https://www.brookings.edu/policy2020/bigideas/the-need-for-civic-education-in-21st-century-schools
11. https://www.americanprogress.org/issues/education-k-12/reports/2018/02/21/446857/state-civics-education/
12. The Civics Project Guidebook supports and promotes meaningful implementation of Chapter 296 of the Acts of 2018, An Act to Promote and Enhance Civic Engagement.

REVIEW QUIZ FOR CHAPTER TWO

1) A civil face to face conversation is a dialogue between two people that intends to build a better _____.
a) understanding b) consensus c) unanimity

2) Civil conversation is _____% speech and _____% non-verbal.
a) 50% & 50% b) 30% & 70% c) 60% & 40%

3) Active Listening is key to Non-Violent Communication (T OR F).

4) Talking-Piece Circle members socialize 80% of the time (T OR F).

5) Modern workplace practices and training developed from and because of the creation of the EEOC in Washington (T OR F)

6) Workplace Conferencing is preferable to mediation when dealing with workplace conflict because it has a narrower focus so that it can pinpoint the problem more precisely. (T OR F).

7) Civic Smarts is shorthand for three essentials needed to be an informed citizen in a democracy: 1) Civic Knowledge 2) Civic Skills and 3) _____.
a) Civic Participation b) Civic Planning c) Civic Dispositions

8) Action Civics are programs that give students an opportunity to participate in _____ to help solve community problems.
a) Essay Contests b) Civic Engagement c) Law Day Ceremonies

9) The late Justice Sandra Day O'Connor was the founder of
a) iCivics b) The Innocence Project c) Cure Violence

10) The Circle Keeper is also a participant in the circle (T OR F)

ANSWERS TO REVIEW QUIZ

1) a) understanding

2) b) 30% speech and 70% non-verbal

3) F

4) T

5) T

6) F

7) c) Civic Dispositions

8) b) Civic Engagement

9) a) iCivics

10) T

CHAPTER 3

RESPONSIVE

PEACE SKILLS

A) Negotiation

B) Conflict Resolution

C) Mediation

    1. Mediation Styles

    2. Six Stages of Mediation

    3. Hybrid Mediations

D) Arbitration

A. Negotiation

Cambridge Dictionary:
the process of discussing something with someone in order to reach an agreement

The authors of *Getting to Yes* define negotiation as a "back-and-forth communication designed to reach an agreement when you and the other side have some interests that are shared and others that are opposed."

Leigh Thompson In her negotiation textbook *The Mind and Heart of the Negotiator*, refers to negotiation as an "interpersonal decision-making process" that is "necessary whenever we cannot achieve our objectives single-handedly."

Max H. Bazerman and Don A. Moore in their book *Judgment in Managerial Decision Making* say, "When, two or more parties need to reach a joint decision but have different preferences, they negotiate."

Negotiation Skills, the first of our Responsive Peace Skills, is as old as mankind. Innumerable articles, courses and books have been written about negotiation styles, strategies, methods, techniques, theories, concepts, and approaches, including those you will find in this book.

ENTER & DO PEACE AGREEMENT

"You do 1 and 3, I'll do 2 and 4"

Principled Negotiation

We highly recommend that everyone at some time take a course in negotiation such as the one offered by Harvard University's Program on Negotiation (PON) which is based upon the four elements of Principled Negotiation. Learning these four elements that are outlined below, as described by Fisher, Ury and Patton in their seminal work Getting *to Yes,* can improve your negotiation skills.[1]

The Four Elements of Principled Negotiation & BATNA

1. Separate the people from the problem

In principled negotiation, negotiators work to deal with emotions and personality issues separately from the issues at stake using active listening and other communication techniques. The goal is not to "win," but to reach a better understanding of each party's concerns.

2. Focus on interests, not positions.

In principled negotiation, negotiators look beyond hard positions and try to identify underlying interests—their basic needs, wants, and motivations. This type of interest-based bargaining can enable solutions that meet each party's needs.

3. Invent options for mutual gain.

In principled negotiation, negotiators devote significant time to brainstorming a wide range of possible options before choosing the best one. In negotiation, options refer to any available choices parties might consider to satisfy their interests, including conditions, contingencies, and trades. For example, imagine a job negotiation where the candidate values time at home with his family, while the would-be employer is concerned about their customer service phone station being fully staffed all five days of the week. If so, the job employer might be willing to make a concession on the number of days the employee can work at home remotely via telephone in return for the promise that he will be answering customer calls whether in the office or at home a full forty-hours every week.

4. Insist on using objective criteria.

In principled negotiation, negotiators rely on objective criteria—a fair, independent standard—to settle their differences. They might agree to abide by standards such as market value or the law. Parties agree in advance as to the objective criteria to consult and agree to abide by them.

BATNA: Best Alternative to A Negotiated Agreement

Parties involved in principled negotiation need to remember their goal is to reach an agreement that would make them better off than their BATNA (*best alternative to a negotiated agreement).* Negotiators work to improve their BATNA both during their preparation and through the course of their negotiations.

The stronger their BATNA, the more they ask for in your current negotiation.

For example, a car buyer might negotiate for two or more vehicles while making a backup plan for alternate transportation if neither of those deals work out. If they and their negotiating counterparts have fully explored their interests and options, there's every reason to walk away from a deal that doesn't meet eithers interests as well as their BATNA does—in fact, it's the right thing for them to do.

VIDEOS ABOUT NEGOTIATION

Anthony Stagg (2011 January 7) Negotiation Skills Top ten tips [Video File]. *YouTube.* Retrieved from https://youtu.be/Oy0MD2nsZVs https://www.youtube.com/watch?v=oy0MD2nsZVs&feature=youtu.be

William Ury (2017 July 25) Getting To Yes With Yourself (93) [Video File]. *YouTube.* Retrieved from https://www.youtube.com/channel/UCQ_xHcpyTuQRfQtAor8GdOw

B. CONFLICT RESOLUTION

We distinguish between the responsive skills used in disputed civil situations such as in the business sphere which we characterize as negotiations with those used to address situations that could devolve into uncivil behavior which we characterize as Conflict Resolution.

We have devised the chart below using the nine letters of our motto WE DO PEACE to illustrate the steps in resolving a conflict which could result from a bullying situation arising at a school, etc.

ACKNOWLEDGEMENT

This chart includes content developed by The Conflict Resolution Network (CRN) in Australia, a network of people with a common commitment to conflict resolution, co-operative communication strategies and related skills located online at: http://www.crnhq.org .

We appreciate and applaud the groundbreaking work that the CRN has done over the decades, not only in Australia, but for that matter all over the world by providing their work product to be used for no other compensation but an acknowledgement such as this.

WE DO PEACE

Anti-Bullying/Conflict Resolution

W - When Bullied or Stressed Take a Breath

E - Elect to Respond, Not React

D - Deliver "I" Statements

O - Opt In For a Win/Win

P - Put On & Walk In Their Shoes

E - Engage Willingly In Workout

A - Admit Your Needs & Fears

C - Create Options Together

E - Enter & Do Peace Agreement

WHEN BULLIED OR STRESSED, TAKE A BREATH

When we are confronted and challenged by a bully or by anyone showing aggressive behavior towards us whether at our school, on our job or in the streets the most important thing for us is not to panic. We prevent panicking by being and remaining calm. The way to become and remain calm is to use the skills of mindfulness, which with the skills of social and emotional learning (SEL) have become increasingly popular.

The most effective calming skill is to concentrate on our breathing by taking deep breaths slowly and purposely. Using the breathing pattern 4-7-8, repeated three times refers to breathing in for four seconds, holding that breath for seven seconds, and exhaling for eight seconds. So, whenever we need to control our emotions, we can do so by simply taking slow, deep breaths, which will in turn lower our heart rate and help us remain calm. Once calm we are in a frame of mind that lets us respond creatively to the aggressive behavior facing us, instead of just reacting instinctively to it.

WHEN BULLIED OR STRESSED, TAKE A BREATH

ELECT TO RESPOND, NOT REACT

When confronted with aggressive behavior our natural tendency is to react quickly to it rather than pausing to take the time to respond to it. Reacting in a panic by either engaging in the conflict or fleeing from it often increases the chances of bringing violence upon ourselves.

If, however, we can respond creatively to this conflict rather than just react to it, we may be able to give ourselves an opportunity to turn a potentially negative event into a positive one. First, while listening to the aggressors vent their emotions center and calm yourself by breathing slowly and deeply. Second, ask them questions to shift their focus away from their anger to exploring the issues. Third, use this exchange to make sure facts and feelings on both sides are mutually understood before addressing each other's needs and fears.

ELECT TO RESPOND, NOT REACT

"Grab the other hose!
Don't just run away!"

DELIVER "I" STATEMENTS

For an encounter to be both meaningful and constructive the parties must deal as equals. You must be respectful of the needs and rights of the other person while asserting your own feelings, needs and ideas. Your being assertive is a healthy attribute and a necessary one when attempting to negotiate a peaceful resolution of a conflict.

"I" Statements or affective statements are a way to tell the other person how their behavior makes you feel or affects you, whether it be either positively or negatively. Delivering an "I" Statement allows you to express your perception of and feelings about a problem without attacking, blaming or hurting the other person. "I" Statements allow you to confidently express your own views and have them heard whenever you choose to assert yourself.

DELIVER "I" STATEMENTS

"I want you to know that I am unhappy with your suggestion".

OPT IN FOR A WIN/WIN

When a conflict appears, you can elect to take one of three options – Fight, Flight or Flow.

1) Fight (Aggressive) = (I Win/You Lose)

2) Flight (Passive) = (I Lose/You Win)

3) Flow (Creative) = (I Win/You Win)

The "Going with The Flow" or "going for the Win/Win" option allows you to respond to the conflict creatively and by doing so share power; not demanding total control, nor surrendering it either. It lets both sides consider not only their own needs and fears, but those of the other side as well thus offering a win/win approach

This approach allows the parties to fashion a peace agreement that's fair to both. Electing this win/win approach is about resisting power, greed, and injustice and by doing so allow all the parties to come out of the conflict winners.

OPT IN FOR A WIN/WIN

PUT ON & WALK IN THEIR SHOES

Empathy is sensing another's feelings, thoughts, or attitudes as if we had experienced them ourselves.

It is being able to communicate to that person our sensitivity to them.

We do not lose our own identity but discover our common humanity by drawing out and being alert to the cues they offer us about their feelings.

We in turn communicate back to them our understanding of their situation as if we had actually "put on and walked in their shoes".

PUT ON & WALK IN THEIR SHOES

"Here's your shoe back. You're right, your shoes are not easy to walk in".

ENGAGE WILLINGLY IN WORKOUT

It is essential that you communicate to the other person your willingness to engage in a workout of the issues constituting the conflict between the two of you. Usually this is not difficult, but there are times when you find you do not even want to deal with the other person or with the problem.

Whatever the reasons for your aversion to engage willingly you must overcome them even if you do not initially understand them. While maintaining the status quo may be comfortable it will not allow you to resolve the conflict and be able to move on.

Focusing inwardly, you can analyze and identify your motivations and by honestly addressing them remove them as impediments to engaging willingly in a workout of the conflict with the other person.

ENGAGE WILLINGLY IN WORKOUT

"Let's work this out"

ADMIT YOUR NEEDS & FEARS

Only by ascertaining the needs and fears of each party to the conflict, including your own, can you come up with a Win/Win solution. Such a solution allows everyone to have as many as possible of their needs (*interests, values, wants*) satisfied and fears (*concerns, anxieties, worries*) alleviated.

By what is called *mapping*, you list the needs and fears of each person in the dispute. You can then ascertain the commonly held needs and fears as well as those that are unique to each party. This provides the basis for seeking ways to resolve the conflict by the parties entering-into a brainstorming session to create possible options. They can then analyze all of them and choose the combination that provides the best win/win resolution of their dispute.

ADMIT YOUR NEEDS & FEARS

CREATE OPTIONS TOGETHER

Options can be created various ways such as by recognizing an obvious solution or by using a trial-and-error approach or by reaching a consensus.

Sometimes current arrangements can be mainly retained by simply adding sweeteners; or by giving to the other party what is valuable for them to receive, but easy for you to give.

For a more complex problem, it may be necessary to clarify it first by "chunking" it into smaller parts and doing more research before the brainstorming for options can begin.

Sometimes it's simply identifying the outcome that the parties agree fulfills most of their needs and remedies most of their concerns

CREATE OPTIONS TOGETHER

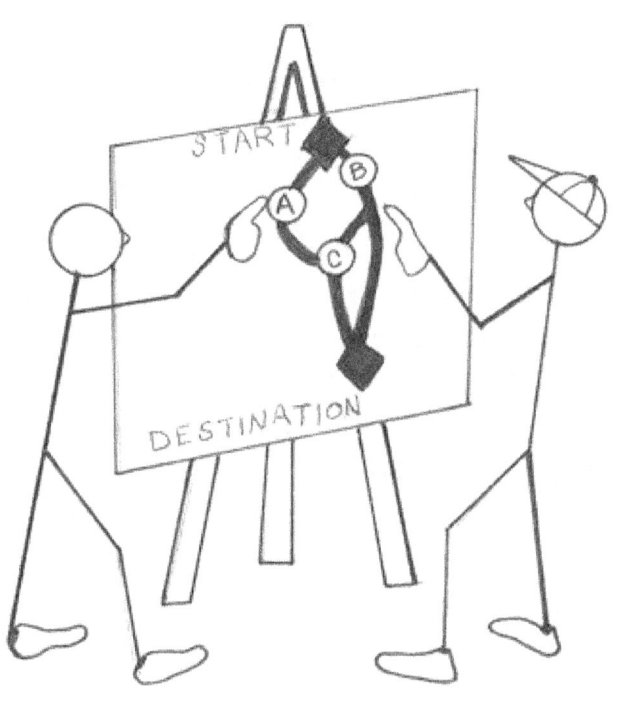

"Which route do you prefer: A, B, or C?"

ENTER & DO PEACE AGREEMENT

Once options are selected, they must be made into a peace agreement, signed, and then implemented. The agreement lists all the tasks to be done, who will do them and when they are to be done. A very important task is for someone to periodically check to make sure that everyone is doing their part in making the peace agreement work as planned.

The nine negotiating skills included in this WeDoPeace Chart provide you with a way to respond to and resolve many kinds of conflict. Please use these skills every day and be sure to share them with everyone you know and meet.

They also form the foundation for learning the other kinds of peacemaking skills that we will discuss in this book, namely mediation and the restorative peace skills like peace circles.

Thank you for learning how to do peace with us.

ENTER & DO PEACE AGREEMENT

"You do 1 and 3, I'll do 2 and 4"

C. Mediation

Mediation is basically an informal negotiation between the parties assisted by a third person called the mediator. Mediation is usually entered into on a voluntary basis, but sometimes mediation is required by a court or by the terms of a business agreement or in the terms of a sales transaction made between the parties. Mediations are non-binding and either side can withdraw at any time. However, once reduced to writing, mediation terms are an enforceable contract in most jurisdictions.

A mediator does not have to be a professional or formally trained to mediate a dispute. Most of us have served in the capacity of a mediator at one time or another, often not even realizing that was the role that we were playing in a dispute between friends. Mediation can be used in all manner of disputes – those between family members, neighbors, business associates, public meeting attendees, even those between nation states.

A mediator is not a judge or an arbitrator so cannot dictate a result; but works with the parties who fashion their own result – one that they believe that they can

MEDIATION
(ONE-ON-ONE NEGOTIATION WITH THE ASSISTANCE OF A NEUTRAL MEDIATOR)

"Thanks for choosing me to be your mediator. Let's get started."

live with that solves their problem without having the expense and inconvenience of a lawsuit. A good mediator is a good listener with good communications skills and empathy so that he/she can paraphrase, clarify, and reframe what is being said so that he can make clear to all listening what speakers are saying and how they feel and what needs they are seeking to satisfy from the mediation.

The mediator sets a time and date agreeable to both parties at a neutral site or online. Usually, the mediator's fee is shared by the parties. Mediation is a quicker and less expensive way to resolve a dispute than going through the courts. Indeed, mediation works so well – about 75% of the time - that most courts require that the parties to a lawsuit must attend mediation prior to going to trial expecting that most of the cases they refer to mediation will resolve within a few hours or a day thus saving the court the time and the expense of a lengthy trial.

A mediator must be able to command some measure of trust and confidence by building a rapport with the parties by honest relationship building during the mediation process. The parties must feel their interests are truly understood by the mediator, because only then will they be willing to accept how he/she reframes their problems and consider whatever creative solutions he/she proposes to them because of reframing. Indeed, many mediators believe that the building of rapport with the mediating parties is even more important than any of the mediation techniques and tactics that they may employ during the mediation process itself. The **mediation process** encourages each side to describe their position regarding the dispute; identify the strengths and weaknesses of their position; understand that there can be no resolution of the dispute without compromise on both sides and **a willingness to** agree on a mutually satisfactory solution.2

Mediation Styles

It should be noted that not all mediators use the same method or style of mediation and that the parties should seek out a mediator who uses an approach suited to the nature of their dispute. If the dispute arises out of a one-time type of business dispute where the parties are not concerned about a continuing business relationship than they might opt for a mediator who uses a directive style geared to bringing the problem at hand to a quick conclusion without regard for the long-term effects of a cut and dry settlement on their relationship with the other party. **On the other hand, those parties seeking to maintain a long-term personal or business relationship would likely prefer to choose a non-directional styled mediator who is more experienced in a transformative mode of mediation.**

Facilitative Mediation

In traditional facilitative mediation, the mediator encourages disputants to work together to reach their own agreement. The mediator does not try to impose his own ideas as to what the solution should look like.

Transformative Mediation

Transformative mediation is akin to facilitative mediation in that it is non-directive with the mediator striving to empower the participants to be able to recognize each other's needs and interests and by doing so provide them with the skills for make transformative changes not only regarding the issue(s) they are dealing with in the mediation at hand; but in the long-term nature of their relationship.

Court-Mandated Mediation

Many court systems have now adopted the use of mediation to increase the number of cases that are settled before trial to save the courts time and money. In some jurisdictions such as Florida, a case cannot go to final trial until after a mediation ordered by the court has been held.

Evaluative Mediation

Opposite facilitative mediation is evaluative mediation, which is usually court ordered. Evaluative Mediators use a directive approach and are usually attorneys who have practiced in the areas of the law that the court assigns them cases to mediate. Their job is to assist each side to assess the legal merits of their position and to evaluate with them the strength and weaknesses of their legal arguments; their likeliness of succeeding or failing at trial in an effort to bring about a settlement between the parties based upon the belief by each party that it can do better negotiating a pre-trial settlement than taking the chance of losing bigtime at trial where their destiny is no longer in their own hands but in those of a judge they may not know.

Virtual Mediation

A mediator no longer needs to meet in-person with the parties at the same location with the advent of online mediation. Telephonic mediation has been used with some limited success in the past when parties were so far apart that it did not make economic sense to travel to an agreed upon mediation location in view of the small amount of money in dispute. Telephonic mediation never caught on as a popular way to mediate cases because of the lack of visual capability to show the reactions of the parties to each other. E-Mail or Online mediation was also unsatisfactory even as it moved from just email exchanges to the early types of video conferencing platforms because there were still technological limitations that made their use quite cumbersome and not as effective as in person mediation sessions.

However, virtual mediation changed that as it came into its own during the Covid 19 Pandemic when in-person mediations were discouraged for public health reasons. By then new and the advance versions of video conferencing services, such as Zoom.us, had been developed with many new and advanced electronic capabilities that allowed mediators to duplicate the techniques that had only been available to them using in-person mediation. Now they were able to share information such as photos, documents, and insurance estimates by using features such as Screen Sharing and Breakout Rooms that electronically created Caucus Rooms, which allowed them shuttle back and forth between the two electronically separated parties. Over time in many kinds of disputes, especially commercially based ones as homeowners' insurance claims arising out of hurricanes and non-weather-related water events, virtual mediation proved in most instances to be as effective as in-person mediation. The new video conferencing platforms allowed the parties to see each other's facial reactions and body language to a degree that had not been possible in the earlier telephone and email versions of remote or distance mediations.

Six Stages of Mediation

Mediation is a multi-stage process that is less formal than a trial or arbitration. Prior to meeting in open session for the first time with the participants to give his opening statement as described below under Stage 1, the mediator may have received letters from some or all the parties describing their positions, concerns, and expectations regarding the upcoming mediation. In addition to the information received in those letters, the mediator may decide prior to the first open session to meet separately with each party to the mediation in person, phone or online to make sure that he/she fully understands the nature of the dispute and all the issues that each party wants to have addressed during the mediation.

The mediator arranges a neutral site and sets a time and date agreeable to both parties. Each side may have multiple participants especially if the dispute is between two companies that include their business leader or representative, company attorney and/or accountant, etc. In addition to agreeing on a neutral place and the mediation schedule the parties need to agree how they will pay the mediator's fees, which are usually split evenly between the parties to the mediation. If they are meeting virtually online the mediator usually selects the videoconferencing platform that all participants will be accessing since it will be the mediator who will be the one operating the platform's controls during the mediation.

Stage 1: Mediator's Opening Statement

At the beginning of the meeting the mediator introduces everyone in attendance to each other and outlines how mediation works in general covering the six stages of the mediation including Joint Sessions, Private Meetings, Negotiating and reaching an Agreement or an Impasse. The mediator also explains specific ground rules such as no verbal abuse being tolerated during the mediation and that only one person can speak at a time during which the others stay silent and do not interrupt the speaker until he/she has finished speaking.

The mediator also spells out the fact that he/she is neutral and impartial; that his/her role is not of a decider but rather of a facilitator. He explains how confidentiality applies to the mediation process and the fact that mediation is a voluntary proceeding that anyone can leave at any time; unless they have been ordered by a court to attend the mediation. At this point the mediator has the option to have a separate meeting with each party to gain a better grasp of what each considers the issues to be dealt with at the mediation prior to having them give their own opening statements in joint session.

Stage 2: Disputants' Opening Statements

Each party is given the opportunity without being interrupted to describe his/her view of the dispute and vent their feelings as to how it is affecting them; and offer up their ideas on how to resolve all or some of the issues making up the dispute.

Stage 3: Joint Discussion

The mediator encourages the parties to join him in asking each other questions about their opening statements to increase their understanding of each other's concerns, needs and feelings; this also lets the participants know that their feelings are being recognized and understood. Also, during this time, the mediator should be using his/her mediation skills to help the parties understand each other by repeating what they have heard the parties say to each other; asking them questions to clarify what each of them wants to achieve from the mediation.

They eventually begin to understand each other's viewpoint and start to focus on resolving a shared problem(s) that exists today but one that they can see is possible for them to eliminate in the future. The mediator using his/her paraphrasing, summarizing and reframing skills assists the parties in understanding each other's concerns and identifying those areas where they agree; and in the process by hearing their feelings being reflected to them in the mediator's words – provides them with the assurance that they and their feelings and concerns are being heard. The mediator should summarize the issues in conflict in a neutral way, so the parties not only agree that they are the points needed to be discussed; but also, in what order- thus setting an agenda for discussions and negotiations.

Once an agenda has been developed the parties should put their attention to the resolving of each issue – many mediators suggest the parties start with the ones where the differences between their interests are not that great. In seeking solution options parties are encouraged to brainstorm so that they can generate a wide assortment of options to choose from in their search for the one that they mutually agree completely resolves the issue in dispute. While this brainstorming exercise should be solely that of the parties the mediator can assist the parties by making sure they all participate and have all been involved in coming up with the agreed upon criteria to evaluate the merits of the options they are generating to resolve the issue at hand.

Stage 4: Private Caucuses

At any time, the mediator can end the joint discussion by separating the parties into separate private caucus rooms. If the joint discussion devolves into emotional personal attacks by the parties on each other the mediator will meet with them privately to continue a constructive exchange of ideas, proposals and offers for settlement. The mediator advises the parties that when they meet with him in caucus whatever they tell him will be held in confidence by him unless they give him permission to share that information with the other side. Often this has the effect of the parties being more forthcoming with the mediator thus allowing him to gain added insight into their overarching concerns and interests. Some mediators never negotiate in joint or open session but use the practice of shuttling between the caucus rooms of the parties as their main means of conducting the mediation – bringing offers and counteroffers back and forth between them; all the while discussing privately with each party the pros and cons of their current negotiating position and the consequences of each offer, they may be making or receiving.

In effect the negotiation is conducted via this kind of "shuttle diplomacy" with offers and counteroffers continuing until there is a full, partial or no agreement to settle the matter. Sometimes a mediator may conduct a portion of the negotiation successfully using the shuttle mode to resolve some of the issues; but then decides to bring the parties back together in a joint discussion or "an open session" in a last-ditch attempt to successfully negotiate a resolution of the remaining outstanding issues.

Either party or his attorney may request that the mediator caucus with them at any time leaving the other party in the main session until they return. The purpose of the caucus may be to share a new offer with the mediator and/or a request that the mediator present the new offer to the other side. Any party can request to caucus with the mediator at any time during the mediation for a variety of reasons. The mediator likewise can ask to caucus with either party during the mediation for any reason again it being understood that the matters discussed are confidential unless the caucusing party gives the mediator permission to disclose the information to the other side.

Stage 5: Joint Negotiation in Open Session

The mediator may have the parties negotiate the entire dispute in open session and never caucus with either of the parties because this is his preferred way of mediating or because he believes it is the best approach based upon the nature of this dispute or the parties involved. On the other hand, the mediator may after the opening statements by the parties place them in separate caucus rooms and shuttle back and forth until the mediation is over; bringing the parties back together at the end to either assist them in drafting a written agreement if there is a partial or complete settlement or to determine if they want to attend further mediation sessions in the event of an impasse or a partial settlement.

Stage 6: Closing

The mediation will either end in an agreement or in an impasse. The mediator may or may not write up the terms of the settlement into a final or even a draft agreement depending upon what the parties and the mediator have agreed to do in this regard. The mediator may do an outline of the terms of the agreement for the parties to take to their attorneys for approval; or may leave it entirely up to the parties to do their own agreement. Usually when attorneys participate in the mediation, they handle the drafting of the agreements. In virtual mediations where there are no attorneys involved the parties may not do a formal written agreement. but memorialize the terms of the agreement in an email exchange that spells out how settlement monies and release documents will be exchanged.

A Short History of Community Mediation

Community mediation can be traced to the Community Relation Service (CRS) established through the 1964 Civil Rights Act to provide a constructive model of dealing with conflict without violence. Another early venue in 1969 was the Philadelphia Municipal Court Arbitration Tribunal supported by the Law Enforcement Assistance Administration with prosecutors and courts offering disputants arbitration hearings to resolve their issues. In 1970, mediation was used to resolve minor disputes in the Columbus Night Prosecutor program. Also at this time, San Francisco's Community Boards Program (SFCB) was established to provide panels of neighbors to resolve disputes within their local communities. Now there are innumerable community and school resources for mediation, dozens of states have court-annexed programs, and NACM has located 650 community mediation resources doing over 50,000 cases a year.[3]

D. Arbitration

Arbitration, like litigation, uses contested trial proceedings to resolve claims before a decider –in litigation in a public court by a judge or a jury, or in litigation in a private court by an arbitrator. We include arbitration in this section of Skills4Peace to show it is a way to resolve disputes when negotiation and mediation fail to resolve them. However, many contested cases avoid having to go to trial at the last minute because they are in fact settled by negotiation or mediation; the former by attorneys negotiating amongst themselves on the proverbial courthouse steps; and the latter by a neutral mediator appointed by a trial judge trying to avoid the time and expense of conducting a court trial. In fact, in some jurisdictions, such as the state of Florida, every case must be mediated by a court approved mediator before it is allowed to proceed to trial.

Arbitration is when the parties failing to be able to settle their dispute agree to a private trail proceeding. Arbitration allows the disputing parties to select an arbitrator of their mutual choice to decide which of them prevails. The arbitrator is paid for by the parties to the dispute. Arbitration, being a form of Alternative Dispute Resolution, is preferred by many businesses over litigation in governmental court systems, because it can commence without inordinate delay upon the parties' agreed upon schedule and its results can remain private and out of the public arena.

Both court litigation and arbitration involve each side presenting evidence in support of its legal position and the decider(s) determining the outcome based upon his/her/their weighing the relevance, materiality, and competence of that evidence. Many business and consumer agreements today contain arbitration clauses that require that all disputes arising between the parties be arbitrated.

Hybrid Mediations

Med-Arb

Med-Arb is a hybrid version of the mediation and arbitration process where first a mediation of the dispute and all its issues is conducted by a qualified mediator. If the mediator is not successful in resolving all or some of the issues, then all the unresolved issues will then be arbitrated by a qualified arbitrator in an arbitration held after the mediation. The arbitration may or may not be the same person who previously mediated the matter depending upon whether that person is also a qualified arbitrator or not. The arbitrator at the conclusion then enters a binding decision on all the unresolved issues. Some observers raise the objection that this process allows the possibility that during the arbitration, the arbitrator may misuse some confidential information that he gained access to because of his previous role as the mediator in the initial mediation phase of this hybrid process.

Arb-Med

Arb-Med is another hybrid of mediation and arbitration that is widely used. A qualified arbitrator first hears the evidence and testimony presented by the parties to the dispute and renders a binding award which he keeps to himself and does not disclose to the parties until after he finishes conducting a mediation of the same dispute with the same parties. If he is successful in mediating the dispute than he does not publish his arbitration award. However. if he is unsuccessful in resolving the dispute during this mediation phase then he finally announces to the parties his previously rendered binding award he reached at the arbitration.

Observers point out that by doing the arbitration first before the mediation the binding award made by the arbitrator cannot be influenced by any confidential information obtained by him/her during the mediation phase since the award is made by him prior to commencing the mediation; and he is not allowed to change his arbitration award because of any new confidential information that he/she may learn in the mediation phase of the process.

NEGOTIATION & MEDIATION COURSES & TRAININGS

The Conflict Resolution Network is a long-time pioneering leader in providing conflict resolution skills education and training to build stronger organizations and more rewarding relationships. All CRN material on its website (crnhq.org) can be freely reproduced provided the copyright notice appears on each page.

The Friends School of St. Paul, Minnesota (https://fsmn.org/about/our-approach/conflict-resolution) This Program is for Grades 1-8.

Peace Foundation of New Zealand
The Foundation's "Cool Schools Peer Mediation Program" is for Primary Schools and its "Leadership Through Peer Mediation Program" is for Secondary Schools. (http://www.peace.net.nz)

The "Peacemaker Program", which has been designed by the Johnson Brothers at the University of Minnesota, allows every student to be trained and to serve as a mediator; not just a few as is the common practice in most other school peer-mediation programs. (Johnson, D. W. & Johnson, R (2005). *Teaching Students To Be Peacemakers* (4th Ed). Edina, Minn.: Interaction Book Co.)

The Peace Center of Bucks County's "Project Peace" is a comprehensive approach to peace education and violence prevention that promotes a safe school environment and encourages optimal learning through academic and social growth. Training is offered to administrators, educators, support staff, students and parents with continued follow-up and support over a three to four-year period. The Peace Center of Buck's County Pennsylvania's Program is for grades 1-12. (http://www.thepeacecenter.org/programs/project-peace-for-schools).

These are all available school programs. They have been successful for decades; for a fee their developers will implement them into other school systems.

The Harvard Program on Negotiation (PON) offers several negotiation and mediation courses, lasting from two to five days, taught by leading faculty and experts in the field. For more information, visit: http://www.pon.harvard.edu/executive-education/

VIDEOS ABOUT MEDIATION

Mediator007 simpleshow (2014 March 24) What is Mediation Anyway? [Video File]. *YouTube* Retrieved from https:/ https://youtu.be/w4s7p7hOjYk

Peerlink07 (2009 February 4) On the Spot Mediation: how to use your skills in everyday life) [Video File]. *YouTube.* Retrieved from https://youtu.be/cIVBtBMmCRo

Popular Mediation and Conflict Resolution Videos (194) [Video File]. *YouTube.* Retrieved from https://www.youtube.com/playlist?list=PL2b2aqjMg8xQCgbjQEkJ6bMeYPwX1

ONLINE COURSES

The Conflict Resolution Network (CRN) Online Conflict Resolution Course. (http://www.crnhq.com)

U OF Michigan Online Course : Successful Negotiation: Essential Strategies and Skills; George Siedel, Williamson Family Professor of Business Administration and Thurnau Professor of Business Law
https://www.coursera.org/learn/negotiation-skills

MEDIATION ORGANIZATIONS

Mediators Beyond Borders International (MBBI) builds local skills for peace & promotes mediation worldwide. MBBI is a recognized service partner of Rotary Int'l.

FOOTNOTES
RESPONSIVE PEACE SKILLS

1. Fisher, R. and Ury, W. (1981) *Getting to Yes.* Boston: Houghton Mifflin.
2. Moore, C. (1986). *Mediation.* San Francisco: Jossey-Bass. (Siedel, G.) Successful Negotiation. Essential Strategies and Skills.
3. Merry and Milner, *The Possibility of Popular Justice*, 1994, and the *Community Resolution Manual: Insights and Guidance from Two Decades of Practice*, 1991.

REVIEW QUIZ FOR CHAPTER THREE

1) A mediator is a third party in the mediation and can decide who wins by agreeing with one of the other two parties (T OR F)

2) A mediation is a _____ proceeding.
a) confidential b) public c) certified

3) In a Med/Arb the mediator and arbitrator are never the same person. (T OR F)

4. The Conflict Resolution Network is based in Australia (T OR F)

5) A Mediator like an Arbitrator admits evidence and decides in favor of one party or the other based upon that evidence. (T OR F)

6) A private confidential meeting between the mediator and one of the parties to the dispute is called a _____.
a) conference b) sidebar c) caucus

7) A mediator is _____.
a) an advocate b) a neutral c) a decider

8) Mediation services are _____.
a) court annexed b) community sponsored c) private businesses d) all the above.

9) A mediation agreement in writing is usually enforceable.
    (T OR F)

10) Impasse means a dispute is _____.
a) settled b) continued c) not settled

ANSWERS TO REVIEW QUIZ

1) F

2) a) confidential

3) F

4) T

5) F

6) c) caucus

7) b) a neutral

8) d) all the above

9) T

10) c) not settled

CHAPTER 4

RESTORATIVE

PEACE SKILLS

A) Affective or "I" Statements)

B) Affective (Restorative) Questions

C) Short & Quick Restorative Chats

D) Restorative Mode Meetings

E) Restorative Justice Circles

F) Restorative Conferences

G) Family Group Conferences

RESTORATIVE PEACE SKILLS

A Peer (Restorative Meeting) Circle

Traditional Justice vs Restorative Justice

In Traditional Justice what are first questions asked?
1. What laws/rules have been broken?
2. 2. Who did it?
3. How should he/she/they be punished?

In Restorative Justice what are first questions asked?
1. What happened?
2. Who has been affected/harmed?
3. What can be done to repair the harm?

Restorative Justice Circles bring victims, offenders, and community residents together in a non-adversarial restorative justice-based process aimed at holding offenders accountable to their victims and community for the damage they have done to them. This approach allows for rehabilitation to replace retribution by giving precedence to repairing the harm done by the offender to the victim and the local community over punishing the offender for breaking the laws of the state.

Restorative Justice allows offenders, who admit their wrongdoing, to enter diversionary programs where they and their victims along with prosecutors and community volunteers can work out agreements whereby the offenders agree to heal the harm they have done to the victim(s) and restore the damage done to the community. If the offenders fulfill these restorative agreements their cases are ultimately dismissed by the Court and their arrest records can be expunged; if they do not their cases will be sent back to Court.

RESTORATIVE PEACE SKILLS

Please note that Restorative Peace Skills like the other peace skills discussed in this handbook are being taught to students in a growing number of school districts. Many districts have found these seven restorative peace skills supportive of the premise that positive behavioral and social skills are central to learning, As a result they have integrated them within multi-tiered behavioral frameworks such as PBIS (Positive Behavioral Intervention and Supports at: https://www.pbis.org) to build a sense of community, improve relationships, and provide a positive alternative to the zero-tolerance exclusionary discipline practices of suspensions, expulsions and in- school arrests which have over the years became known as "the school to prison pipeline".

We call this positive alternative approach to school discipline "Restorative Discipline" because we see it as a student centered and a student-run Restorative Justice-based self-disciplinary system. It provides the entire school community with the peacemaking skills needed to resolve on-campus conflict in a peaceful and respectful way.

Where Restorative Discipline has been adopted it has shown that it results in an improved school climate allowing for more students staying in school, earning better grades, and graduating on time. So please keep in mind that the Restorative Peace Skills described in this section are not only being taught to students, but in many schools, they are also being used by those same students as they participate in a school-wide Restorative Discipline Program to discipline their fellow students who break school rules.

These seven Restorative Peace Skills, derived from Restorative Justice are now often referred to as Restorative Practices, when used outside the judicial arena. They can be ranked as to degrees of formality and complexity. They range from informal and relatively simple (A) Affective or "I" Statements, (B), Affective or Restorative Questions (C) Short & Quick Conversations or "Chats", to the semi-formal and more structured (D) Restorative Mode Meetings to the most formal and complex (E) Restorative Justice Circles(F) Restorative Conferences and (G) Family Group Conferences.

A. Affective or "I" Statements *	(Informal)
B. Affective or Restorative Questions	(Informal)
C. Short & Quick Restorative Chats	(Informal)
D. Restorative Mode Meetings **	(Semi-Formal)
E. Restorative Justice Circles	(Formal)
F. Restorative Conferences	(Formal)
G. Family Group Conferences	(Formal)

*[Affective or "I" Statements, which were part of our discussion of Negotiation earlier in this chapter, deal with our being able to express our feelings in response to the positive or negative behavior of another person. "I" Statements or "I" Messaging was created and developed by Dr. Thomas Gordon, a famous 20th Century American psychologist
**[Restorative Mode Meetings are when Talking-Piece Circles which are usually social in nature about 80% of the time are used in their Restorative mode to deal with disputes arising between their own members perhaps 20% of the time]

A. Affective or "I" Statements

Making these inter-personal statements allow people to express their feelings and build relationships because they become more human, accessible, and empathetic. They also allow people to talk about a behavioral situation without assigning blame – they provide the way to be able to separate the deed from the doer.

The format of an Affective or "I" Statement is:

"I feel/am_____(emotion)____when/that you _____(behavior) _____".

Or

I feel/am_____(emotion)____when/that you _____(behavior)___because____(reason)_____."

An example of an Affective or "I" Statement is:

"I am unhappy when you interrupt me in mid-sentence"

Or

"I feel unhappy when you talk about how great the zoo outing was because you promised to take me with you."

B. Affective or Restorative Questions

Posing Restorative Questions is a language skill that when properly used can provide the Victim, (a/k/a the Impacted or Affected Party) the opportunity to find out why they were harmed, to have a voice and be heard; and be a part of developing an agreed upon solution that includes the Offender that will repair the harm done to them and prevent it from happening again.

The following questions are generally used to question the victim(s)[1]:

1. "What happened and what was your reaction at the time of the incident ?"

2. "How do you feel about what happened ?"

3. "How has this affected you?"

4. "Who else was affected and how ?"

5 "What would you like to see happen to repair the harm done to you and prevent it from happening again?"

Likewise, other Restorative Questions allows the Offender (a/k/a Responsible or Accountable Party) to reflect on the impact of their behavior upon the victim(s); develop a degree of empathy for the victim and provides them the opportunity to be part of an agreement with the victims to repair the harm that they have done and to prevent it from happening again.

The following questions are used to question the offender(s):

1. "Tell us in detail what happened?"

2. "What were you thinking about and feeling at the time?"

3. "How has this event affected you?"

4. "Who else do you think has been affected by your acts and how?"

5. "Is there anything you want to say now?"

6. "What do you think can be done to repair the harm & prevent it from ever happening again?"

C. Short & Quick Restorative Chats

A short restorative conversation or "chat" is usually used to solve an immediate issue in the moment, most anywhere and can be used on a one-on-one basis or for a few or a handful of participants. Whatever issue(s) involved need to be approached with an open mind to:

1. Truly understand what happened.

2. Authentically listen and provide a space where everyone authentically listens to one another.

3. All voices are heard.

4. Focus on the impact the situation/actions had on others and the larger community.

5. Identify any unmet needs (especially for those harmed), and

6. Determine what needs to happen to make things as right as possible moving forward.
   (For more information go to this source: http://www.healthiersf.org/RestorativePractices/Resources).

D. Restorative Mode Meetings

Restorative Mode Meetings are when a Talking-Piece Circle (discussed above on page 43 under **Group Circles**) that is eighty (80 %) percent of the time convened for social reasons and to build trust amongst a group of people is called together into a meeting in which it meets only 20% of the time in its restorative mode to respond to a conflict between two or more of its members – it deals with less serious incidents of wrongdoing than those that would be referred to the more formal Restorative Justice Circle, Restorative Conference or Family Group Conference which are discussed in the next section of this chapter.

Restorative Mode Meeting participants, who all know each other, understand that they are there because of a conflict has arisen between the parties and that restorative questions dealing with the conflict will be at the center of the meeting's agenda instead of the usual trust building type questions that constitute a typical meeting of their Talking-Piece Circle.

A generic outline for a **Restorative Mode Meeting** for resolving a conflict within a Talking-Piece Circle is provided below. Note that it is in step 8 that the Restorative Mode Questions for the conflict at hand are introduced.

GENERIC OUTLINE - FOR A RESTORTATIVE MEETING CONVENED FOR RESOLVING CONFLICT.

START THE MEETING
1- Circle Keeper & Guardian Arrive
2- Announce Purpose of Circle is to resolve conflict
3- Open Circle With An Opening Ceremony
Drumming, Singing Chanting Praying Or Quotations.
4- Review The Standard Guidelines For All Circles
5- Create Or Update Agreements Of This Specific Circle

DO THE MEETING
6- Check-In Round Question Using The Talking Piece
i.e.: *What is your name and how to you feel ?*
7- Do Community or Trust Builder Round(s)
i.e.: *What do people like about you best?*
(See More Questions from U of Maryland Law School)5
8 - Ask Restorative Questions For This Conflict
9. - Reach Consensus Agreement On All Issues
10 - Write Up & Sign the Restorative Peace Agreement
11 - Check-Out Round Question
i.e.: *What is your take away from this circle ?*

COMPLETE THE MEETING
11- Close With A Closing Ceremony
12- Host A Post Gathering For Refreshments
13 –Do Check-Ups To Monitor RJ Agreements

E. Restorative Justice Circles

The guiding principles of restorative justice are:
1. An offense is against human relationships.
2 Victims & community are central to justice process.
3. The first priority is assisting victims.
4. The second priority is to restore the community.
5. The offender has a personal responsibility to victims and community for offenses committed.
6. Stakeholders do restorative justice as partners.
7. Offender develops better competency and understanding.[2]

Justice Circles may involve participants who have been referred by a criminal, juvenile, a special purposes court or another government department such as child welfare. Indeed, there is a world-wide trend of increased usage of peace circles in the criminal justice system especially in the juvenile justice arena. This growing trend is the subject of an article entitled "Peacemaking Circles: A new tool for juvenile court?"[1] which shows how the circle process is being introduced: "Peacemaking circles use traditional circle ritual and structure to create a respectful space in which the crime victim, victim supporters, offender, offender supporters, judge, prosecutor, defense counsel, police, court workers, and all interested community members can speak in a shared search for understanding the event at issue; participants also identify the steps necessary to address the harm caused by the offense and to prevent future occurrences. The peacemaking circle process typically involves several steps that lead to the sentencing. An application by the offender to the circle process is followed by the creation of a support system for the offender and a support system for the victim. Other steps are a healing circle for the victim and healing circle for the offender. These steps are then followed by the sentencing circle. After the sentencing circle, there may be follow-up circles at appropriate intervals to review progress on the sentencing agreement. The circle process is not simply a process for finding more appropriate justice; it is an exercise in building community, because it brings community members together in a forum that allows exploration of the underlying causes of crime and encourages each community member to offer gifts or capacities to the process of finding solutions and implementing them. The circle process allows full expression of emotions and channels the energy of those emotions toward positive solutions. In the circles, decisions are based on consensus, and everyone involved must agree that the decision is one with which they can live. Circles draw on the life experiences of all the participants to understand the problem at hand and to devise workable solutions."

Restorative Justice Facilitator's a/k/a Circle Keepers will partner with state attorneys, police, and courts by conducting facilitated Restorative Justice Conferences with victims, offenders, and affected stakeholders to repair harm and hold both youthful and adult offenders accountable for their bad behavior and choices.

Also by adopting Skills4Peace, schools will be able to use their students who have been trained in doing peer circles to change over to a student centered and student run "Restorative Discipline" approach to school discipline thus ending for good the failed zero-tolerance discipline policies of arrests, suspensions and expulsions of the past, a/k/a "the school to prison pipeline" that have accelerated the flow of minors into the criminal justice system . These restorative justice-based circles are designed to treat students with typical teenager behavioral problems in ways that will allow them to be accountable for their misbehavior and be reconnected to the school community again and not driven out of it. However, students exhibiting behavior that is either self- endangering or is a danger to others must be referred to the administration for help. (https://restorativeworks.net/2014/10/chicago-fights-school-prison-pipeline-restoratively)

Restorative Justice is being used to reform juvenile and criminal justice systems worldwide by using sentencing circles in the court systems; and using re-entry circles in corrections departments for releasing prisoners from jails and prisons back into resettlement communities. The goal is to add the input of the community into both the justice and corrections systems by including community volunteers in both kinds of these circles. Research shows that the restorative justice approach, which is often used in victim offender dialogue programs, increases victim and offender satisfaction, decreases offender recidivism, and increases the rates of restitution as compared to the traditional criminal justice process.[3]

Sentencing Circles

Sentencing circles or accountability boards as they are also called are composed of volunteers from the community who along with law enforcement and prosecutors are invited to be circle members. The sentencing circles seek to keep the healing and repair of the victim and the community along with the rehabilitation of the offender as the focus of the process; not the punishment of the offender as has been the practice in the past. It should be noted that all sentencing circles or accountability boards are not the same since their composition and scope of applicability will reflect the political and cultural preferences of the governing bodies that create them.[4] To date while most jurisdictions enacting restorative justice sentencing circles have restricted their use to low tier offenses and for first time offender cases; there are increasing studies and calls for determining their effectiveness and applicability to more serious offenses.

Felony & Domestic Violence Cases

Ironically, the only known use of restorative justice sentencing circle in a murder in the United States took place in the state of Florida, a very conservative criminal justice jurisdiction where the use of restorative justice is virtually non-existent.[4] However, an ad hoc restorative sentencing conference was held in a case of homicide in the Second Judicial District of Florida in Tallahassee. This one-of-a kind restorative conference was held at the prodding of the parents of the victim who had been fatally shot by her boyfriend.5

This restorative justice sentencing circle or conference was done during what was scheduled to be a pre-plea conference usually attended only by the prosecutor and defense attorney for the purpose of trying to arrange a plea deal which is then brought to the Court. In this case the conference was expanded to include a facilitator, the victim's family, the offender's family, the offender himself and a community member. It should be noted that the sentence that was submitted to the Court was not one that was arrived at by a consensus of all the participants as might usually be expected to happen at a restorative sentencing circle. Everyone did have the opportunity to speak including the victim's parents, who had early on forgiven their daughter's killer. While the prosecutor did not adopt the exact term of years the parents of the victim had wanted, it was apparent that their wishes did not go unheeded.

There is a question in many societies especially in the US and the UK about the applicability of restorative justice to certain types of cases namely, domestic violence, intimate partner violence, sex offenses and hate crimes. The fear of those dealing with domestic violence victims is that their offenders will be able to use and leverage the practices of restorative justice to continue to be able to coerce and terrorize their victims.

Authorities in the UK do not want there to be any distinctions as to the ages of victims and offenders who can access restorative justice services in the country nor for there to be a denial of access to those services based upon the nature of the crime visited upon a victim by an offender. They nevertheless explicitly discourage police from pressuring victims of domestic violence and sexual offenses into accessing their local restorative justice services suggesting that these victims should not be provided such services unless they are being facilitated by those with specialized restorative justice training in these sensitive areas of domestic abuse, intimate partner violence and sex offenses.

In the US, most who work in the domestic abuse area share the belief that offenders must remain in the traditional criminal justice system. They also believe that if restorative practices are to be made accessible to the victim that they be offered to them in parallel with and not as an alternative to traditional criminal justice remedies. Others, such as Professor Leigh Goodmark, supports is an advocate for the viewpoint that the Violence Against Women Act (VAWA) should fund more of the Restorative Justice approaches to the problem along with the existing Criminal Justice approaches.6

The UK government has embraced restorative justice across the whole breath of its criminal justice and prison systems all-across the country including Scotland and

Wales. They also consider restorative justice youth services in Northern Ireland to be a model system for the rest of the country probably because facilitator training required there is measured in weeks compared to a matter of days in the rest of the UK.

It should be noted that the on the ground application of restorative justice in the UK is uneven, not only between England & Wales, Scotland, and Northern Ireland, but also within each of these three jurisdictional sectors. There are some places such as Gloucestershire in England where governmental and non-governmental agencies right across the county have all embraced Restorative Justice and support and offer a whole spectrum of restorative services while in other places within England perhaps only the police provide a basic restorative service; some with and some without dialogue between victims and offenders.[7]

While there is not a national law or governmental policy that is well funded insuring universal availability of Restorative Justice services in the UK, there is an unofficial national Victim's Charter of victim's rights which In Section 1 Standard 1.3 calls for every victim when reporting a crime to be advised by the police as to where they can obtain information about Restorative Justice Services. Take note that this standard is not a requirement that these services must be provided to every victim reporting a crime that wishes them; but just that every victim reporting a crime must be given information about the availability of these services. (https://www.nidirect.gov.uk/articles/victim-charter)

As in the United States the definition and application of Restorative Justice varies by jurisdiction. Restorative Justice Services provided by the police of one UK jurisdiction may mean an actual dialogue that has been mutually agreed to between the victim and offender after the conviction and before the sentencing, or after the sentencing; while in another jurisdiction what is called Restorative Justice is not that at all but more like a mediation where the victim and offender never meet face to face or even communicate directly via mail or email, but rather are provided an intermediary in the form of a police officer.

This policeman, operating more in the fashion of a shuttle-style mediator than a restorative justice practitioner or facilitator, may offer to try to get the victim restitution in whole or in part from the offender (while he is also getting the offender to also do some community service), but never offers to get for the victim what is the one thing of real value from restorative justice process to the victim which is a mutually agreed to face to face meeting (or other direct mode of communication between the victim and the offender such as email) so that the victim knows that: he/she is actually being heard by the offender; the offender is taking full responsibility for his/her criminal act; and the offender actually offers to repair the harm done and tries to make things right for the victim, the community and also for the offender him/herself, as well, in respect to achieving rehabilitation and full integration and acceptance back into the community.

Prison Programs

Restorative Justice Programs are being used in prisons in many jurisdictions in varying degrees. In the United States as of 2015 there were twenty-seven states where victims or their survivors of all kinds of crimes including those of murder were meeting face to face with their offenders in prisons who they had either victimized them or their loved ones. These meetings are often either called Victim/Offender Dialogues (VOD) or Victim/Offender Mediations (VOM). The dialogue is victim-centered between a prepared consenting victim and his/her prepared consenting offender assisted by a trained facilitator or mediator. The purpose is to facilitate a healing process for both the victim and the offender by giving them an opportunity to meet in a safe, secure structured face-to-face meeting.

Prison programs include the widely used Sycamore Tree faith-based one. Like most prison programs it does not involve direct meetings between victims and their own offenders - it brings prisoners together with a group of surrogate victims instead. These surrogate victims describe to the prisoners how they felt by being victims of a crime at the hands of another offender; this promotes awareness amongst the prisoners of the harms to victims and promotes empathy towards victims. The consensus is that this surrogate process while not providing perfect closure is nonetheless a healing process for both the prisoners and the victims.

The UK provides support to its prisons which choose to establish Restorative Justice Programs. As a matter of fact, the country's premier professional RJ provider membership association group - The Restorative Justice Council that sets professional service standards has given HMP Leeds prison its converted RSQM (Restorative Service Quality Mark) designation. This designation, developed in collaboration with the Ministry of Justice, assures participants in the Restorative processes of its designees, that they are receiving safe effective service.

Based upon the number of providers meeting the six standards of service, the RJC has established safe, high-quality delivery of Restorative services all-across the country not only in the Justice sector, but in the education and social services sectors by serving the welfare of families and children as well. The Restorative Justice Council website declares that its vision is of a society where high-quality restorative practice is available to all. (enquiries@restorativejustice.org.uk).

The biggest hurdle for widespread usage by prisons of the RJ process is the difficulty of finding and arranging for in prison conferences because of a variety of complications, even for those victims eager to participate in the process: lack of resources such as insufficient prison staff and systemic data sharing barriers; some victims delay face to face meeting until after the offender has served the full prison sentence so as to avoid suggestions the prisoner took part in RJ only as a way to try to shorten his/her sentence; not being truly accountable nor sincere in their claims to want to repair the harm done to the victim and make amends to the community.

A growing program known as the Insight Prison Project was founded in 1997 with one class for 14 male prisoners at San Quentin State Prison. It offers transformational programs for prisoners and parolees, which are supported by crime victims and community volunteers. IPP currently conducts 25 weekly classes at San Quentin State Prison, involving some 300 prisoners, as well classes in 15 other prisons in California, and Colorado, three county jails, several reentry facilities, and one juvenile institution. Its curriculum of courses helps inmates to develop the ability thru insight to have a clear perception of their situation and by having learned the skills of awareness, emotional intelligence and critical thinking be able to avoid impulsive behavior and make conscious choices that can be the difference in reoffending or not. These three skills are similar to those in the Formative and Responsive Peace Skills categories of Skill4Peace.

Reentry Circles

Restorative Justice also employs the use of Reentry Circles for assisting both juvenile and adult prisoners reentering the community upon completing their sentences. Residents of the community, such as members of neighborhood circles, volunteer to participate along with corrections and probation officials on these reentry circles. This provides community input in arranging for resources to be marshalled to support the reintegration of these offenders into the community making the chance of recidivism less likely.

The Bureau of Justice Statistics reports that in 2007, more than 7 million people in the U.S. were incarcerated, on probation, or on parole, one in every 31 adults, with 2.2 million of them in prison or jail. Ninety-Seven (97%) percent of prisoners currently in prison will someday be released, and approximately 600,000 are released every year with more prisoners returning home having spent longer time behind bars. Many inmates are ill-prepared to enter community life, and few have effective family and community supports in place to ease the reentry.

Two states in that have embraced Restorative Reentry Circles to take on the responsibility of people reentering their communities and providing them with the support and accountability they need to become productive, law - abiding, responsible citizens are Vermont and Hawaii.

According to studies by the Pew Center, one (1) in forty-six (46) Vermont adults is under corrections supervision. Restorative Reentry Programs run by Community Justice Centers across Vermont promote the principle of "no more victims". 8

By establishing and enforcing clear expectations of its participants for positive community behavior, restorative reentry interrupts the cycle of criminal offending. In Hawaii, an innovative facilitated reentry circle process for youth and adults called Hulkahi Restorative Circles was introduced in 2004 and uses a public health approach which applies both Restorative Justice Circles and Solution-Focused Brief Therapy (SFBT), which is goal-oriented, and strength based.9

Vermont's Restorative Reentry Programs work with people, who have committed serious and violent offenses and have been released or are about to be released from prisons, to help them successfully reenter their communities. A key component of their comprehensive reentry program is what they call Circles of Support and Accountability (COSAs).
These are groups of three to four trained citizen volunteers who meet regularly with a "core member"-- the person reintegrating following a prison term -- for at least the first year of his or her reentry. COSA volunteers provide emotional and practical support to help the core member become a productive self-supporting citizen. The COSA concept comes from a proven program of the Mennonite Central Committee

of Ontario to provide "radical hospitality" to people, who in the absence of community support and accountability, were likely to reoffend, thereby creating safer communities. Prospective "core members" are screened to assure that they are appropriate candidates for this program. Before release, core members begin the process by working with their prison case worker, a probation officer & the local Community Justice Center staff to create a plan for transition to community life.

Vermont also has Restorative Justice Panels for Reentry program participants who

- Have identifiable victims
- Need to learn about or are ready to make amends for the harm s/he caused

Participants will meet with a volunteer community panel and victims who are interested in participating to deepen their understanding of the harm they caused and try to make amends. Both the Vermont and Hawaii programs offer Family Reintegration Conferences to people who seek a different, more positive relationship with family members and/or friends with whom they will have contact upon release from prison.

Typically, these conferences are conducted before a person is released and are designed for people who

- request permission to live with family or friends

- have victimized family in the past
- have family members who have expressed concerns about the impending release.

They meet in prison with loved ones who they identify and are invited by the circle facilitator. Often the circle is the first time the imprisoned person has seen some members of their family for months or years. The imprisoned person's needs addressed include how they might make amends for any harm that their behavior and imprisonment may have caused their loved ones and the community at large.

Other needs addressed during the circle include housing, transportation, finding a job, creating and living within a budget, taking responsibility for one's past actions by making amends for past offenses, how emotional and physical health can be maintained by getting help for mental or emotional problems such as addiction, depression, learning disabilities and any other needs identified by the imprisoned person, e.g. obtaining any necessary documents, getting a divorce, continued learning, etc. A prison staff person usually participates in the process.

A detailed written plan with concrete steps and timelines is prepared after the circle and provided to the circle participants. Follow up circles are provided as requested by the imprisoned person. The process is being replicated in California, Washington DC, and a women's prison in New York. The circles have also been used for people completing parole and probation, and a new project will test the process for people entering federal prison in Hawaii.

Circles have been provided for imprisoned people who were innocent yet convicted and incarcerated under the rule of law. In these circles, the innocent imprisoned person's harm was also addressed restoratively.

Note: Hawaii Friends of Restorative Justice has conducted 134 circles with 575 participants who have completed surveys about the process including measuring increased optimism that stronger social bonds were created or strengthened for the imprisoned person during the circle. 100 of the surveyed participants found the circles were positive even in cases where the imprisoned person who had a circle became re-incarcerated. Research also shows children of incarcerated parents have experienced "healing" quantified as increased hope about the future (optimism) and decreased rumination over past traumatic events (forgiveness). Preliminary research also shows promise that the circles help decrease recidivism.

A GENERIC OUTLINE FOR A "JUSTICE CIRCLE"

A/K/A "RESTORATIVE CIRCLE"

START THE CIRCLE:

1 - Circle Keeper & Guardian Arrive
2 - Announce the Purpose of Circle Is Restorative
3 - All Parties and Community Members Seated
4 - Open All Circles With An Opening Ceremony
5 - Review Standard Guidelines Of All Circles
6 - Create Or Update Agreements Of Circle

DO THE CIRCLE:

7 - All Circles Do Check-In Round With Talking Piece
8 - All Circles Do Community Building Round(s)
9 -- A series of questions to offender then to victim:
.
To person doing the harm (The Offender):

1 What happened?
2 What were you thinking at the time?
3 What have you thought about since?
4 Whose been affected by what you did?
5 In what way?
6 What do you need to do to make things right?
7 How can we stop this from happening again?
8 What can we do to help you?

To person who has been harmed (The Victim):

1. What happened?
2. What did you think when it happened?
3. What have you thought about since?
4. How has it affected you?
5. What's been the hardest part for you?
6. What's needed to make things right?
7. How can we stop this from happening again?
8. What can we do to help you?

10 - All the participants are asked the above questions

11 - Check- Out Question Asked Of All Participants:

What have you taken from being in this circle and how do you feel?

CLOSE THE CIRCLE

1 - Close All Circles with A Closing Ceremony

2 - Post Circle Social Gathering with Refreshments

3 - Post Circle Check-ups to Monitor RJ Agreements

VIDEOS FOR RESTORATIVE JUSTICE IN COURTS POLICE, CORRECTIONS & RE-ENTRY

Pete Lee (2012 September 25) Colorado State Representative Pete Lee on Restorative Justice [Video File]. *YouTube*. Retrieved from https://youtu.be/rFMyHaGo49Q

Restorative Solutions (2014 November 20) Restorative Justice Conference [Video File]. *YouTube*. Retrieved from https://youtu.be/7xE8pIdoZNg

RJ@VictoriaUniversity (2015 Swptmber 29) Leigh Goodmark Keynote Two: Domestic Violence and Restorative Justice [Video File]. *YouTube* Retrieved from https://youtu.be/kX3p9yqLhy8

RJColorado.org (2010 October 19) Restorative Justice In Justice Systems [Video File]. *YouTube* Retrieved from https://youtu.be/R9tl4YmYYnI

TEDxTalks (2015 April 8) Undefinable Relationship | M. Gunderson & S. Pessinguia WashingtonCorrectionsCenterforWomen [Video File]. *YouTube* Retrieved from https://youtu.be/2ZtjkE0-5tA

Brave New Films (2016 September 13) Restorative justice Why Do We Need It? [Video File]. *YouTube*. Retrieved from https://youtu.be/8N3LihLvfa0

VIDEOS FOR RESTORATIVE JUSTICE IN COURTS POLICE, CORRECTIONS & RE-ENTRY

Communities for Restorative Justice (2014 May 15) Police Perspectives on Restorative justice Circle Process [Video File]. YouTube Retrieved from https://youtu.be/_hBUpJNpzaQ

Restorative Justice Center (2014) Restorative Dialogue for Severe Violent Crimes (Three Cases) by Mark Umbreit [Video File]. Vimeo Retrieved from https://vimeo.com/111252683

Restortive Justice Center (2014) Twelve Videos [Video File]. Vimeo Retrieved from https://vimeo.com/crjpvideos

RETN (2014 March 5) Vermont's Innovative Restorative Reintegration Strategy [Video File]. YouTube Retrieved from https://youtu.be/ZKpbdxXA2FI

Heart Phoenix River (2014 April 2) Phoenix Center For Peacebuilding [Video File]. YouTube. Retrieved from https://youtu.be/zCVfPMCbaVA

heartspeak (3007 July 2) Restorative Justice Continuum –

Howard Zehr Ph.D EMU[Video File]. YouTube. Retrieved from https://youtu.be/2KXwnbsQUrI

Center for Court Innovation (2016 July 22) Restorative Justice: Panel at Community Justice 2016 [Video File]. YouTube. Retrieved from https://youtu.be/jZTSmARqD7c

F. Restorative Conferences

A Restorative Conference is the most formal of the six Restorative Skills and is used to address the most serious incidents of wrongdoing. It is victim centered so that the primary emphasis is on repairing the harm done to the victim. This is in marked contrast to our traditional legal and discipline systems where the main focus is on punishing the offender with little if any participation of the victim in the proceedings. Victims who agree to participate in a conference are able to speak to their offender(s), express their feelings and have those feelings acknowledged by their offender(s) who must take responsibility for their part in the incident before they can participate in the conference. Since other members of a community, whether it be neighbors, schoolmates, or fellow workers, are often involved in the incident they are also invited to participate in the restorative conference since in addition to being punished the offender needs to be reintegrated back into that community after he or she has achieved a resolution with the victim.

The purpose of the conference is to foster empathy in the offender(s) as they hear how their actions have affected the victim(s), the victim's supporters and their own friends and family. For a conference to be successful, extensive pre-conference preparation is required by the facilitator(s), who needs to have been trained in conducting a formal restorative conference. The facilitator must speak to all the parties involved, confirm their participation, and explain the conference process to all the participants beforehand.

The physical setup for the conference is to create a circle of chairs with the offender(s) and their supporters on one side of the facilitator and the victim(s) and their supporters on the other side. The goal at the end of the conference is an agreement between the parties as to how the offender can make restitution for the wrongs done both to the victim and to the community. The conference facilitator follows a "Conference Facilitator's Script" like the generic one on page 58 or the one created by Terry O'Connell, which he has provided free to all restorative conference facilitators world-wide.1

Once an agreement has been reached between the parties the conference is concluded by all participants sharing in the refreshments, which begins the reintegration of the offender(s) into the community. The restorative conference can either be used in lieu of traditional punishment or as a supplement depending upon the type, severity, and sector of society where the wrongdoing occurs. In the educational sphere it is often in lieu of punishment except in very serious acts such as those of violence and law breaking; whereas in the judicial sectorial it is employed more commonly as an alternative to prosecution for lower tier; but not so much for serious criminal cases such as felonies; although recently in New Zealand it is being used for some felonies in some of their Community Group

Conferences. It is increasing being used more widely in prisoner reentry into local settlement communities.

There are various models of conferencing that have been developed since the 1990's that are being used in various parts of the world today. All of them to be successful require a shift in the role of the juvenile justice official from that of being the sole decision maker to acting as a facilitator of community members participating in the decision-making process; and to also act as a resource to assist those community members in their new decision-sharing role.

When the outlines of a restorative justice practice were just beginning to emerge fifty years ago there was some overlapping with mediation, terminology-wise, probably because the first circle keepers of facilitators were usually mediators. Thus, for example the term Victim-Offender Mediation has been used in some places for restorative justice. Today in most jurisdictions the word mediation is no longer used when referring to aspects of restorative justice having been replaced by either the word "conferencing" or "dialogue".

Mediation skills are employed only in response to a conflict or dispute already existing between parties as compared to restorative skills which can be used to prevent wrongdoing by the building of strong trusting relationships amongst group members; and used to also deal with someone who has harmed a member of the group. Mediating parties usually have very little interest as to which of them is right or wrong. They just want to resolve the dispute and move on. However, establishing who did the harm is essential in the circle process since the healing cannot start until the offender admits he did the wrong to both the victim and the community. This act of taking responsibility by the offender begins the process of repairing the harm he has done to the victim and the community. It not only heals the victim and the community but allows the offender to make things right in a way agreeable to everyone including the offender himself; eventually allowing him a pathway back into the good graces of the community.

Various conferencing models being used include the Restorative Conferencing f/k/a Victim-Offender Mediation (United States and Europe since the mid-1970's) in the courts and the corrections arena; Circle Sentencing (Canada – Colorado & Massachusetts since 1992); and the Reparative Boards in Vermont.

While the amount of time and degree of complexity to do conferencing with these models varies, all of them are much more time consuming than the other forms of restorative peace skills such as the delivering affective ("I") statements, asking restorative affective questions, engaging in impromptu restorative "chats", or doing a restorative mode meeting. Following is generic conference facilitator's script as an example of same.

A GENERIC CONFERENCING FACILITATOR'S SCRIPT

STEP 1: Welcome, my name is NOF (Name of Facilitator) and I have been asked to facilitate this meeting.

(Now Introduce all the participants and their relationship to the victim or wrongdoer) I have spoken to all of you about the incident (briefly outline what happened).

WD1 (wrongdoer's name) has admitted his/her/their part in this incident. You are all gathered here to discuss what happened, not to discuss or decide the character of anyone involved.

I will ask each of you to talk about how you and others have been affected by what happened. This will help everyone to understand what needs to be done and how each can be a part of repairing the harm and putting things right.

STEP 2: (Begin by addressing the wrongdoer/s WD1): "I would like to start by asking WD1 "Can you tell us about what happened and how you became involved?"

"What happened next?" (Continue asking this question until their story is complete)

"What were you thinking at the time?"

"What have your thoughts been since?"

"How has this affected/upset you and others?"

"What's been the hardest thing for you?"

STEP 3: (Addressing the harmed victim V1) – I would like to start by asking V1:

"Can you tell us about what happened and how you became involved?"

"What happened next?" (Continue asking this question until their story is complete)

"What were you thinking at the time?" "What have your thoughts been since?"

"How has this affected you and others?"

STEP 4: (Address to each of the remaining participants the same questions)

STEP 5: (Go back to the wrongdoer/s and ask): "Now that you have just heard how V1 and the others have been affected - Do you see the harm that has been caused by what you did?"

"Is there anything you want to say at this stage?"

"Do you think that something needs to be done to repair that harm and put things right?"

STEP 6 (Return now to the harmed victim/s and ask) – "What do you think needs to happen?"

STEP 7: (Go back to wrongdoer/s W1 and ask) "What do you think of what V1 has suggested?"

STEP 8: (Return to V1 and his/her supporters and ask them) "What do you think about what has been said?" & "What would you like to see come out of today's meeting?"

STEP 9: (Go back to Wrongdoer W1 and ask) "What do you think about what has been said?"

STEP 10: Now have the participants suggest what needs to be in the contractual agreement having the wrongdoer/s agree to each one before writing it in and discussing the next one. After all terms have been written into the agreement add in the deadlines and whose responsibility it shall be to monitor that the timelines are being met. Read each provision out loud checking to see all agree and then ask each of the participants to sign the agreement.

STEP 11: A final invitation to speak – Ask if there are those who want to say something before the meeting is closed –"Before I close this meeting is there anyone else who wishes to say something?"

STEP 12: Close the meeting – Thank everyone for participating in this meeting and invite them to partake of the refreshments and socialize together before they leave.

G. FAMILY GROUP CONFERENCE

The Family Group Conferencing Model originated in New Zealand at the behest of the Māori indigenous peoples who were dissatisfied with the way the courts were treating their young people in criminal and social welfare matters. In 1989 the government of New Zealand borrowing from the traditions of the Māori replaced going to court with the aboriginal practice of convening the extended family of the youth to develop a plan to address these type problems. It adopted the practice nationwide making it applicable to all its youth by calling it Family Group Conferencing and incorporating it into its Children, Youth and Families Act of 1989; thus, beginning a revolution that started its spread to juvenile and criminal justice systems around the world.

Two years later in New South Wales Australia, a community policing sergeant in the city of Wagga Wagga by the name of Terry O'Connell took the New Zealand model which was originally designed for use by social workers and adapted it by creating a script which his fellow police officers could use in their policing efforts. His script reflecting his approach differed from the New Zealand model in that it omitted a mandatory family alone time that did not include the other participants - what is called the "family caucus feature". Through Terry O'Connell's tireless efforts his script has been widely adopted first in his native Australia, then the UK and finally in the United States where he met and became associated with Sharon and Ted Watchel, founders of the International Institute of Restorative Practices (IIRP), located in Bethlehem PA. 1

The purpose of the conference is to foster empathy in the offender(s) as they hear how their actions have affected the victim(s), the victim's supporters and their own friends and family. For a conference to be successful, extensive pre-conference preparation is required by the facilitator(s), who needs to have been trained in conducting a formal restorative conference. The facilitator must speak to all parties involved, confirm their participation, and explain the conference process to all participants beforehand.

The physical setup for the conference is to create a circle of chairs with the offender(s) and their supporters on one side of the facilitator and the victim(s) and their supporters on the other side. The goal at the end of the conference is an agreement between the parties as to how the offender can make restitution for the wrongs done both to the victim and to the community. The conference facilitator follows a "Conference Facilitator's Script" like the generic one on page 58 or the one created by Terry O'Connell, which he has provided free to all restorative conference facilitators world-wide.1

Once an agreement has been reached between the parties the conference is concluded by all participants sharing in the refreshments, which begins the reintegration of the offender(s) into the community. The restorative conference can either be used in lieu of traditional punishment or as a supplement depending upon the type, severity, and sector of society where the wrongdoing occurs. In the educational sphere it is often in lieu of punishment except in very serious acts such as those of violence and law breaking; whereas in the judicial sectorial it is employed more commonly as an alternative to prosecution for lower tier; but not so much for serious criminal cases such as felonies; although recently in New Zealand it is being used for some felonies in some of their Community Group Conferences. It is increasing being used more widely in prisoner reentry into local settlement communities.

1 Note: The Terry O'Connell script is from the Conferencing *Handbook: The Real Justice Training Manual* written by Ted Wachtel, Terry O'Connell & Ben Wachtel. The script is provided to all facilitators worldwide without modifications for running their own conferences via a download from the Real Justice website at: (www.realjustice.org/pdf/script.pdf.) IIRP Graduate School (2016 August 16) Introduction to Conferencing [Video File]. *YouTube.* Retrieved from https://youtu.be/BFYm17wF2Iw

A Commentary Upon the Victim's Role in Traditional vs Restorative Justice

All victims are little more than unpaid extras in a long running melodrama staged by the State to prosecute their offenders; but many victims take the opportunity to elevate their roles to that of bit players by electing to deliver centerstage their own authored statements of condemnation of those they often have never met prior to or since the offense. Their moment in the limelight over, they take their unanswered questions back home with them putting them away taking them out only periodically to polish them along with the silverware.

Restorative justice on the other hand takes the victim and the offender, with their permission of course, out of their separate courthouse green rooms and makes them and their supporters leading figures in a new theatre-in the-round production.

A classic tale of redemption and forgiveness scripted to provide them with scenes of a shared humanity allowing them to meet and learn about each other; scenes of empathy where they recognize the needs and emotions that have driven the acts of the other; scenes of character development as offenders transform their fantasies of responsibility into reality by actually entering into agreements to repair the harm that they have visited upon their victims; and finally scenes of celebration culminating in a finale where all the players singing in unison link arms with each other and then with the members of their audience. All of them now joined in rejoicing in the reconnection of all the torn threads of their communal fabric that had been pulled apart because of the offenders' actions against their victims. Healing divisions and restoring unity, the community now welcomes back home the offenders once again as full-fledged citizens as it continues to enthusiastically embrace the victims who having no unanswered questions at all - keep on singing.

Walter Sylvester 2021

VIDEOS ABOUT RESTORATIVE PEACE SKILLS

Resolve Consultants (2017 June 10) Introduction To Restorative Approaches [Video File]. *YouTube.* Retrieved from https://youtu.be/gJJxbn1VjYo

Camp Stomping Ground (2017 February 18) What Restorative justice? Let's Restore Our Broken System) [Video File]. *YouTube.* Retrieved from https://youtu.be/lq554Oxc8js

TEDx Talks (2017 November 30) Restorative justice Laila Fakhoury [Video File]. *YouTube.* Retrieved from https://youtu.be/MSy-qOiYjrA

TEDx Talks (2014 January 26) Restorative Justice Mara Schiff [Video File]. *YouTube*. Retrieved from https://youtu.be/Q4B89j3MrEA

Pinellas County Schools (2017 November 7) Restorative Practices Video File]. *YouTube*. Retrieved from https://youtu.be/oby3a-Rfkxs

NASSPtv (2013 November 20) Restorative Practices: Impromptu Meeting [Video File].*YouTube*. Retrieved from https://youtu.be/q1io7YH2yTU

RJColordo1 Restorative Justice in the Justice Systems [Video File]. *YouTube* Retrieved from https://youtu.be/R9tl4YmYYnI

Edutopia (2014 July 4) Restorative Circles (35 Videos) i.e., Using Dialogue Circles To support Classroom management [Video File]. *YouTube*. Retrieved from https://www.youtube.com/watch?v=qTr4v0eYigM&list=PL1gL_4lwpGh0zS5228azIlxaQl2FgnR4L

Chicago Public Schools (2014 July 18) A Restorative approach To Discipline [Video File]. *YouTube*. Retrieved from https://youtu.be/5r1yvyP141U

Restorative Justice (In Schools) 31 videos [Video File]. *YouTube*. Retrieved from https://www.youtube.com/playlist?list=PLmj5xoVUw2Em2aGCfcfgid_a-5ZNWU4Ly

Paul Bogush (2011 Nov 20) Middle School Fishbowl Di9scussion [Video File]. *YouTube*. Retrieved from https://youtu.be/RwxnBv-dNBIFourth is Team or Workplace

Cassidy Friedman (2013 April 22) Restorative Welcome & Reentry Circle [Video File]. *YouTube*. Retrieved from https://youtu.be/uSJ2GPiptvc

River Falls Community Television (2015 March 9) SCV Program PSA 0315 [Video File]. *YouTube*. Retrieved from https://youtu.be/https://youtu.be/v7DPfEJODtg

MettaCenter (2018 August 13) Anew Story of Justice: Nonviolence and Restorative Justice [Video File]. *YouTube*. Retrieved from https://youtu.be/0YMxk3v7mVY

Restorative Justice Council (2015 April 16) Moving On [Video File]. *YouTube*. Retrieved from https://youtu.be/fWtFtWY3Hh8

Restorative Resource (2015 April 28) The Animated Intro to Restorative Justice [Video File]. *YouTube*. Retrieved from https://youtu.be/rE7rPahe38I

StMattsTosa(2015 January 29) Restorative Practices/ Circle Keeping [Video File]. *YouTube*. Retrieved from https://youtu.be/5FUItXPUEpU

RestorativeCircles(2009) Dominic Barter On Restorative Justice [Video File]. *YouTube*. Retrieved from https://youtu.be/o-AUwX61-34

Edwin Rutsch (2012 September 20) +Jay Pranis & Edwin Rutsch: How To Build a Culture of Empathy with Circle Process [Video File]. *YouTube*. Retrieved from https://youtu.be/Mj8feRbZSAQ

RESTORATIVE SKILLS COURSES & TRAININGS

CDI Restorative Practices Training Programs
In Ireland the Childhood Development Initiative (CDI) offers introductory training in Restorative Practices and Restorative Practices Facilitation Skills. (www.twcdi.ie)

International Institute of Restorative Practices (IIRP) in Bethlehem, Pennsylvania is an accredited graduate school offering one 30 credit Master of Science degree and one 12-credit Graduate Certificate. IIRP also provides trainings & workshops in facilitating of Circles & Restorative Conferencing. (iirp.edu)

Little Friends For Peace of Mt. Rainier, Maryland offers Peace Camps, after-school clubs, in-school classes for youth as well as Peace Circles, training, workshops & the Peace Academy for adults. (http://www.lffp.org/)

River Phoenix Center for Peacebuilding
in Gainesville, Florida offers classes, workshops and trainings in restorative practices and provides services. (http://www.centerforpeacebuilding.org/)

Washington County, Minnesota Community Circles
Circle 101 Training in the values, principles, and components of the Circle process. Circle Keeper Training is also available. (https://www.peacemakingcircles.

FOOTNOTES - RESTORATIVE PEACE SKILLS

1 Barton AB. Peacemaking Circles: A new tool for juvenile court? [Internet] Atlanta, BA: Georgia State University College of Law; [cited2014 Feb 21]: http://law.gsu.edu/dyarn/fall06/law7062/Peacemaking%20Circles%20-%20ABA%20Presentation%20Materials.htm
2 http://www.nij.gov/topics/courts/restorative-justice/Pages/welcome.aspx
3 http://restorative justice.org
Victim Offender Communication in Felony Cases: an analysis of Ohio's office of victim services dialogue program by Donna and Jan M. Bortobn (May 2009 Article 9129).
4.Section 985.155, Florida Statutes, permits the state attorney for each judicial circuit in Florida to establish a Neighborhood Justice Center for operating a deferred prosecution program for first-time, nonviolent juvenile offenders. A handful of judicial circuits have opted in.
5 http://www.nytimes.com/2013/01/06/magazine/can-forgiveness-play-a-role-in-criminal-justice.htm
6. https://academicworks.cuny.edu/clr/vol18/iss1/17
7. http://www.restorativegloucestersire.oo.uk
8 cjnvt.org
9. hawaiifriends.org
10. a public-private partnership that includes the U.S. Justice Department's Bureau of Justice Assistance, The Pew Charitable Trusts, the Council of State Governments Justice Center, the Crime and Justice Institute, the Vera Institute of Justice, and other organizations
11. Urban Institute, *Justice Reinvestment Initiative Report* http://www.urban.org/sites/default/files/alfresco/publication-pdfs/412994-Justice-Reinvestment-Initiative-State-Assessment-Report.PDF

REVIEW QUIZ FOR CHAPTER FOUR

1) Family Group Conferences are exclusive to New Zealand where they are available just to the indigenous people. (T OR F)

2) The first Restorative City in the world is Hull in the UK. (T OR F)

3) Many school districts are replacing the "school to prison pipeline" with restorative practices disciplinary programs. (T OR F)

4) The first Victim Offender Mediation and first Sentencing Circle both occurred in Canada. (T or F)

5) Restorative Justice prioritizes repairing the harm to the victim and community over punishment of the offender. (T OR F)

6) The three informal restorative peace skills are "I" Statements, Restorative Chats, and Family Group Conferences. (T OR F)

7) The one semi-formal restorative peace skill is Restorative Mode Meetings the others being either informal or formal. (T OR F)

8) The Circle Keeper runs a circle like a judge runs a courtroom – with an iron hand. (T OR F)

9) An offender to be permitted to enter a Restorative Justice program must first take responsibility for his/her wrongful acts. (T OR F)

10) Restorative peace skills are not called Restorative Justice but are called Restorative Practices when they are used in non-judicial venues such as schools and business. (T OR F)

ANSWERS TO REVIEW QUIZ

1) F

2) T

3) T

4) T

5) T

6) F

7) T

8) F

9) T

10) T

CHAPTER 5

CURATIVE

PEACE SKILLS

A. The Medicine Wheel

B. Healing Circles

C. Holistic Circles

D. Primary Care Circles

E. Trauma-Informed Care

F. Mental Health Programs

G. Anti-Violence/Delinquency

H. Drumming Circles

A. The Medicine Wheel

The four stages of the peace circle have also been described by some circle keepers using language that mirrors the four points of the medicine wheel as interpreted by some native people as compared with aspects of our beings i.e., body, heart, mind, and spirit.[1] Native peoples share the belief the Medicine Wheel must be in balance. Kay Pranis analogizes this to striking a balance in the circle process by stating that the circle keepers need to spend as much time on meeting and building trust amongst participants as on addressing issues and developing plans of action.[2]

In her 2003 working paper for the New Zealand State Services Commission[3], Lynne Dovey explained the connection between peacemaking circles and the Medicine Wheel based in part upon the work of Carolyn Boyes-Watson, whom Dovey cites in her paper:

"The Medicine Wheel symbolizes a holistic view of human life where body, mind, emotion, and spirit are the four quadrants of the wheel or circle. The interconnectedness of these four aspects of life is overlaid on a holistic view of the four seasons, the four cycles of life (infancy, adolescence, adulthood, and old age), the four essential elements of the earth (wind, fire, rain, and earth), the four directions (north, south, east, west) and the four races of our planet.

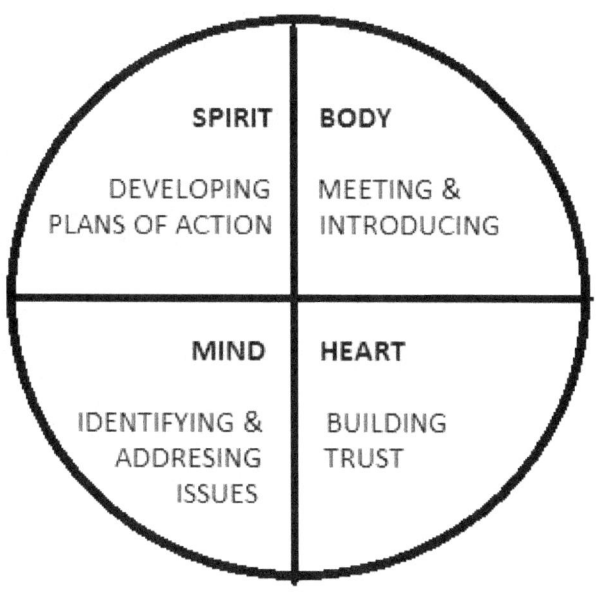

Body (Meeting & Introducing)

Heart (Building Trust)

Mind (Identifying & Addressing Issues)

Spirit (Developing A Plan of Action)

The teachings hold that each of these elements is a part of a whole, an essential part of our natural existence, and each is held in balance with each other around a sacred fire. In many Native American cultures, a person who is acting out or harming others is "out of balance"; if one person is out of balance, so too is the community. Similarly, the understanding in a circle is that a problem for one is a problem for all. We are all connected, and the wisdom of the circle teaches us that we all must move to restore balance. **No one person - no problem - is ever put in the middle of the circle for all to blame, judge, to correct, or even to help"** (Boyes-Watson, Carolyn, Healing the Wounds of Street Violence, CYD Journal, Volume 2, No.4, Fall 2001, pp 16-21).

B. Healing Circles

The circle has always been a place for healing. Native North Americans have always considered their Medicine Wheel as a sacred space in the visible world where healing of Mother Earth and all her species of plants minerals and animals, including humans, was made possible by the protective spirit of each species which exist in the invisible world unseen by us, working in concert with the Creator to heal by using ceremony, meditation, contemplation, and prayer. While there are specific healing ceremonies, all kinds of ceremonies are considered to have innate healing qualities since they are the means that the Creator working thru the spirits gathers and sends healing powers of the Universe thru whoever is conducting the ceremony to benefit those not well.

All ceremonies share common elements such as those of cleansing, and centering. Cleansing is accomplished by smudging which is using the smoke from burning herbs such as sweet grass, tobacco, sagebrush, or cedar to cleanse the energy field of a person, place, or thing. Centering is the means that all the energy of the creation is centered in our bodies and gives us the healing and help that we need.[4]

There are a variety of traditional ways to center oneself in a ceremony including drumming, rattling, chanting, being aware of the sights and sounds of nature around you, as well as concentrating and paying attention to your breath, which brings us full circle into the present-day trending of the use of Mindfulness across the globe. These means of centering oneself can be used to center members of a group as well as an individual with the breathing exercise being done for optimal energy flow by joining hands in a circle preferably with left palms up and right palms down.

A specialized form of modern healing circle that has been developed is one that seeks to support those who are fighting diseases, such as Cancer and Alzheimer's in their own way; as well as those dealing with grief over the loss of a loved one. The approach taken is to offer support to one's fellow circle members who are dealing in their own way with their afflictions or grief. Healing Circles are also formed for caregivers of those afflicted. These circles do not claim to cure the afflictions of their participants nor do circle members try to suggest or recommend a way to " fix" the problems presented by their fellow circle members, but rather to always be there - to listen to each other and support each other as each of them continues to work on and deal with their respective challenges as he/she sees fit. In the United States Michael Lerner Co-Founder of Commonweal located in Bolinas California has been instrumental over decades in pioneering this healing circle concept and in influencing its growth by supporting those launching similar type Healing Circles in Langley, Washington on Whidbey Island and in Houston Texas.[5]

C. Holistic Circles

Another type of circle that is being adopted by a growing number of hospitals and health treatment facilities is a holistic one to complement traditional treatments particularly in the cancer fighting arena. They are creating these healing circles to add psycho - social components to their existing treatment regimens of surgery and chemo to create a holistic treatment model with which to serve their patient.

One such program called BOLD (Bronx Oncology Living Daily) located at the Einstein School of Medicine in the Bronx in New York has also developed a BUDDY mentoring program that pairs cancer survivors as mentors for patients just starting their surgery or chemo treatments. It creates individualized programs of services and activities based upon ongoing assessments of patients' interest and needs.6

Holistic Circles such as developed by the BOLD Program at Einstein which initially form as Talking type circles diversify over time in form and function to cater to the varied needs and desires of their growing membership. This results in an expanded and diversified array of social activities being offered which allows the program to appeal to and serve an increasing number of patients with activities that can range from drum circles to crocheting circles to dance, painting, and creative writing circles.

D. Primary Care Circles

While most healing circles are complementary to traditional western medicine there are situations arising where doctors are looking at the role that healing circles could have within the mainstream practice of traditional medicine. A key example of this innovative approach is the subject of a study reported in the 2014 Spring Edition of The Permanente Journal.8

Dr. Lewis Mehi-Madrona MD. PhD, MPhil reported in his article entitled <u>Introducing Healing Circles and Talking Circles into Primary Care</u> the results of his case study of implementing healing circles within conventional primary care to learn whether outcomes could be improved.7 The 1211 participants in these circles were asked to focus on drugs, alcohol, and mental health in the respective native communities; and how community members could work together to solve these problems. Following are conclusions of his case study stated by the doctor, who uses the terms Healing Circles and Talking Circles interchangeably:

"Limitations of this current study must be acknowledged. Perhaps anything that enabled people to sit together for four or more times would show high levels of effectiveness, although this would potentially be one of our points: that people sitting together and talking about the ordinary problems of life may be as beneficial or more beneficial than consulting the general practitioner. Certainly, we cannot say that the talking circle format is the cause of the changes observed since there was no control group, but we can suggest a beneficial effect of bringing people together with a structure that allows them to speak and be heard. Preliminary data from another study underway suggest that the effect size for change for clients receiving conventional psychiatric care in the US is small (Mehl-Madrona, manuscript under editorial review, 2014).
The clients in our study experienced large effect sizes. We should, therefore, walk through the door of exploring peer-to-peer support and mutual help in primary care and, of course, aim to make primary care even more culturally appropriate to the population it serves.

The circles were peer-led after the first introductory circle. Peer leaders were not paid, and participants were not charged. Thus, the cost-benefit ratio is potentially favorable. Professionals were not involved except to initiate the circle. The initiator's attendance was not required for these circles to continue. After the first session, the only costs were that of heating and lighting the building. Effect sizes equaled or exceeded what is seen for other common interventions in primary care and/or mental health care. Circles or similar peer-counseling interventions may have an important role in these days of escalating health care costs. They provide an opportunity for people to help each other without reliance on professional expertise. Talking/healing circles or other forms of peer support and/or peer counseling could become a useful adjunct to conventional health care. . . Further research is warranted to determine the acceptability of talking circles or more generic peer counseling groups to broader population groups. Talking circles could potentially reduce health care costs by providing a low-cost forum for people to manage and to resolve stress-related and other life problems"

E. Trauma - Informed Care (TIC)

The "ACES" study conducted by the Centers for Disease Control and Kaiser Permanente in the mid-1990's focused on how traumatic childhood events may negatively affect adult health. It documented how common adverse childhood experiences are across all populations and it provided the basis for identifying the different types of traumas and their impact in a person's childhood development, in later life situations and in present-moment interactions.[8]

The "Aces" study led to the training of practitioners with trauma-informed Care skills. These trained practitioners understand how adverse childhood experiences can influence trauma victims in later life; allowing them to apply their professional help to those people seeking to experience self-expression with enhanced emotional safety; while at the same time being able to identify those who as children were able to cope, recover and effectively adapt to trauma on their own; thus, becoming Trauma Resilient.

"Vicarious Trauma" is an occupational hazard for those working in victim services such as restorative practice practitioners who are continually interacting with victims of trauma and violence. On the other hand, "Vicarious Resilience" can have a positive influence on those same practitioners resulting from their exposure to the resilience of those for whom they serve.

F. Mental Health Programs

a) Typical or Troubled Teen educates and trains high school teachers, coaches, bus drivers, and other school personnel about the warning signs of mental health problems (http://www.americanpsychiatricfoundation.org/what-we-do/public-education/typical-or-troubled)

b) Teen Mental Health Literacy Project

The Canadian Pathway through Care is an evidenced-based method to increase mental health literacy linking health care services to schools where young people are.

http://www.mhinnovation.net/organisations/teenmentalhealthorg & http:/www.jordanbinionproject.org

G. Anti-Violence/Delinquency Programs

Cure Violence is an anti-violence program that approaches violence as an infectious disease and that can be combatted as an infectious disease epidemic. http://cureviolence.org/

b) Youth & The Law is our civics-orientated module to help reduce juvenile delinquency and foster student-run self-disciplinary school programs; improve police-student cooperation and teach youth their rights and responsibilities as citizens in a constitutional democracy.

H. Drumming Circles

In the high desert of Joshua Tree California, Master Percussionist Daniel Ray, the legendary hand drummer, professionally known as Big Black, periodically presents his "Environmental Rhythms" concerts and workshops at The Harrison House of Music, Art, and Ecology. Over the decades, this unique performance venue has been developed under the guidance of Director Eva Soltes into a premier international destination and residence for musicians, artists, and thinkers; thus, honoring the work and memory of its multi-talented designer- the innovative composer Lou Harrison.[9]

These drumming workshops of Big Black bring us full circle to the holistic powers of the Medicine Wheel. These healing powers generated by Creation are accessible to all of those who are in sync with the percussive vibrations of these environmental rhythms. The drumbeat helps us to center, balance and connect our innate life energy with the spiritual powers of the Unseen World; powers which protect, preserve and heal humans and all other creatures on this earth from afflictions that arise in all four directions and on all four points of the Medicine Wheel - Physical, Mental, Emotional & Spiritual.

VIDEOS FOR CHAPTER FIVE - HEALING CIRLCES

The New School at Commonweal (2016 May 22) What is a Healing Circle [Video File]. *Vimeo*. Retrieved from https://vimeo.com/newschoolcommonweal/hc-what

The New School at Commonweal (2016 May 22) Circle Agreements [Video File]. *Vimeo*. Retrieved from https://vimeo.com/newschoolcommonweal/hc-agreements

The New School at Commonweal (2016 May 13) Introduction to Healing Circles [Video File]. *Vimeo*. Retrieved from https://vimeo.com/newschoolcommonweal/hc-introThe

New School at Commonweal (2016 May 21) Circle Roles [Video File]. *Vimeo*. Retrieved from https://vimeo.com/newschoolcommonweal/hc-rolesThe

New School at Commonweal (2016 May 21) Preparing a Circle [Video File]. *Vimeo*. Retrieved from https://vimeo.com/newschoolcommonweal/hc-preparing

Einstein School pf Medicine (2017 May 16) A BOLD New Approach to Living with Cancer in the Bronx [Video File]. *Youtube*. Retrieved from https://youtu.be/NcY-GkdjJuU

Einstein School pf Medicine (2017 May 16) A BOLD New Approach to Living with Cancer in the Bronx [Video File]. . *Youtube* Retrieved from https://youtu.be/NcY-GkdjJuU

Barry Winfred Bailey (2010 July 28) Medicine wheel teacher. series part 1 [Video File]. *Youtube* Retrieved from https://youtu.be/cQ32re5c-AI

Barry Winfred Bailey (2010 July 29) Medicine wheel teacher. series part 2 [Video File]. *Youtube* Retrieved from https://youtu.be/RsW44zfdNlo

nouredinephotography (2007 May) BIG BLACK_ORGANIC ORCHESTRA [Video File]. *Youtube*. Retrieved from https://youtu.be/PexJ8exsQnA

BigBlacksPage (2010 December 8) Big Black on, "Environmental Rhythms" [Video File].*Youtube*. Retrieved from https://youtu.be/ZgylxXnxiuU

Waltwayne (2010 July 10) Being Big Black [Video File]. *YouTube*. Retrieved from https https://youtu.be/EqpiGfB5t7k

Eva Soltes (2017 March 24) Lou Harrison Discusses His Opera "Young Caesar". [Video File]. *YouTube*. Retrieved from https://youtu.be/xWiwfLBtyBY

REVIEW QUIZ FOR CHAPTER FIVE

1) Four points on Medicine Wheel - Spirt, Body, Heart, and Soul (T OR F)

2) Centering centers _____ in our bodies giving us healing we need.
a) Energy of All Creation b) Heat of the Sun c) Wisdom of the Elders

3) Holistic Circles add psycho-social components to existing treatment cancer regimens such as surgery and chemo (T OR F)

4) Modern healing circles are designed not only to support their members but also cure or "fix" their ailments.

5) Trauma Informed Care practitioners understand how adverse childhood experiences can affect trauma victims late in life (T OR F)

6) The APA program educates school personnel in the warning signs of mental health problems. (T OR F)

7) CURE is an anti-violence program that is based upon the belief violence is an infectious disease curable by fasting. (T OR F)

8) One study showed healing or talking circles could be a feasible, economical alternative to primary care provider visits. (T OR F)

9) "Vicarious Trauma" is an occupational hazard of those interacting with victims of trauma and violence. (T OR F)

10) Hand drummer Daniel Ray's concept of Environmental Rhythms is based upon the centering of all of the energy of creation (T OR F)

ANSWERS TO REVIEW QUIZ

1) F – Spirit, Body Heart, and Mind.

2) a) Energy of All Creation

3) T

4) F

5) T

6) T

7) F

8) T

9) T

10) T

FOOTNOTES
CURATIVE PEACE SKILLS
1. Sunbear, Wind W, and Mulligan C.(1991) Dancing With The NATIVE AMERICAN MEDICINE WHEEL: Comparison In Life Posted By Jamie K Oxendine April 8th, 2014 Blog NATIVE AMERICAN MEDICINE WHEEL: Comparison In Life Posted By Jamie K Oxendine April 8th, 2014 Blog http://www.powwows.com/native-american-medicine-wheel-comparison-in-life/Wheel, New York, New York: Fireside Simon & Shuster.

2. Pranis K. (2005), The little book of circle processes. A New/Old Approach to Peacemaking, Intercourse: Good books. Little Books of Justice & Peacebuilding.

3. Working Paper 16. Author Lynne Dovey: State Services Commission, September 2003 Working Paper: Achieving Better Social Outcomes in New Zealand Through Collaboration: Perspectives from the United States https://www.ssc.govt.nz/node/7918

4. Bear S, Mulligan C &Wind W. (1992). *Dancing With the Wheel* New York Simon & Schuster.

5. https://www.healingcircleslangley.org

6. https://www.einstein.yu.edu/centers/cancer/support/fundraiser/mission/

7. Mehl-Madrona, (Spring 2014) Introducing Healing Circles and Talking Circles into Primary Care. The Permanente Journal.18(2)4.

8. https://www.cdc.gov/violenceprevention/aces/about.html

9. https://louharrisonhouse.org

Epilogue

This book is our collection and categorization of what we believe are the essential and basic peace skills that are as necessary for mankind's survival as knowing how to find shelter, food, and water. All the knowledge in the world whether practical, academic, or technical is of little value in a community with a disconnected citizenry existing in a culture devoid of civility and empathy that is victimized by unceasing chaotic fits of violence.

On 21 November 2016, the newly appointed ACT Attorney-General, Gordon Ramsay gave the opening address to a Workshop in Canberra, Australia entitled "Restorative Practices in the Criminal Justice System". He emphasized the importance the ACT Government attached to the concept of restorative practices: *"Restorative practice is something that is the foundation of a global social movement. It is not just a latest fad. It is something that is sweeping through and carrying us and allowing new perspectives. Restorative practice implies the use of restorative principles: the principles such as participation, accountability, fairness, inclusion and shared problem-solving. These principles help to build trust and equitable relationships between people so that we can create a peaceful and productive workplace and beyond. Restorative practice is an important reminder to us that we don't live in an economy where the aim is to balance the books and to* get enough assets to balance out the deficit, but instead we live in a community based on relationships and the aim is for all people to have the opportunity to live a decent life".

His predecessor, Attorney General Simon Corbell, said "We tend to think about restorative justice as only applying to the domain of justice, when in fact we could be thinking and asking questions about what a restorative-approach would look like in the places we live, learn, work, play and pray. What would restorative approaches look like in our processes - in human resource management for instance, on our university campuses, in our directorates when dealing with each other, as colleagues or with those who are at the receiving end of our work? What might our sporting and recreational clubs look like if we adopted a restorative philosophy and starting position?"[1]

We urge each you to learn the basic peace skills in this book, teach them to your children and apply them in your daily interactions with others across all sectors of your community. Endeavor by doing so to help make your community into a restorative city much like the people of Hull, Leeds, and Bristol among others in the UK; Tallaght, South of Dublin, and a growing number of cities across Ireland; Canberra and Newcastle in Australia; Whanganul on the West Coast of New Zealand; Nova Scotia are doing; and as some in

Vermont, Minnesota, Colorado, Oakland and Detroit within the USA have begun to do.

Mark Finnis, a leading Restorative Practice Consultant in the UK, who has extensive experience of implementing restorative practices in a range of local authorities around the UK including the Cities of Hull and Leeds, which are the world's first two restorative cities, respectively, wrote in an article entitled <u>Towards a Restorative City, County, Authority or Community</u>[2]:

"The ultimate-goal is the adoption of restorative values and principles to inspire communities to feel empowered to shape their own futures. This is aimed at providing communities with the confidence to resolve their own problems and generate their own set of community values.

Professionals, children, families and all need to spend time investing in their own social capital, being proactive in capitalising on relationships and putting the repair of harm and relationship breakdowns as a key priority. . . At a time of shortage, resources need to be focused on responses to offending or wrongdoing that are efficient, effective and which meet the needs of victims and harmed persons, communities, and our wider society.

This must be a multi-agency cross service approach involving criminal justice, education, social care, housing, police, health, voluntary sector, and all other key partners. There are more and more areas around the country embracing this way of working, some of which I have had the pleasure to be involved in and this can only be exciting for the country-as-a-whole. Just be careful though - it's not just about just having a vision to become a restorative community, city, county, or authority. After all, a vision without action is just hallucination." (markfinnis@mac.com).

There is not yet one universal model for establishing a restorative city or county or country. There are however community-wide programs that have evolved over the past decade or so starting with the ones in Hull and Leeds in the UK. For example, there is a brilliant one, started in Tallaght, just south of Dublin, that is now spreading across Ireland. This innovative Irish program which is outlined in a guide for implementation entitled "A Community-Wide Restorative Practices Programme: Implementation Guide" was created by the Childhood Development Initiative (CDI) Dublin might just become model for developing restorative cities beyond the boundaries of the emerald isle.[3] A YouTube video of this program's implementation is instructive for those seeking information on how to start such a program.[4] There is also an evaluation of the program available done by the UNESCO Child and Family Research Centre at the University of Ireland, Galway.[5]

"On the other hand, a universal "Restorative City Model" may never evolve on the global level because of cultural and societal differences; but as the above quote from Mark Finnis states there is no question that there are basic "restorative values and principles" for all cities to adopt to resolve their own problems, generate their own set of values and shape their own futures.

We believe that he is also correct in that any community seeking to achieve restorative city status must do so on a multi-agency cross service approach of all the key partners within the community that he describes – education, social welfare, criminal justice, housing, police, and the public health and voluntary sectors. We list education first because we not only believe that it is the most important agency in his list, but we also choose to do so in a broader sense as well – while the school system is key in keeping restorative practices going; education in the home is just, if not even more, important in the creation and building of a restorative city.

All human violence is based upon our behavior and what each of us choose to do to express our emotions and needs – beginning at home – not only is it about children's behavior but it is also about what behavior their adult parents choose to exhibit in handling and expressing their own emotional needs. It seems that all child psychologists emphasize how important it is for parents to model the behavior they want their children to use. So, the pre-school years are as important as any in laying the foundations of a restorative society, let alone a restorative city.

That is why our Skills4Peace Framework rests upon the parents first modeling the formative peace skills of Mindfulness and Social and Emotional Learning. Parents, first with the guidance of their pediatricians and child psychologists, must begin inculcating these basics of positive behavior at home prior to formal schooling; but must then willingly become full partners with their children's Pre-K educators in getting and keeping their children aboard our Skills2Peace Initiative. Our educational initiative, presented to children as a metaphoric train ride full of learning and training in the skills of peace, will successfully carry them thru their childhood years all the way to their high school graduations and beyond.

Our Skills2Peace Initiative integrates the formal educational years into the overall lifelong Skills4Peace Framework. Integration is the important aspect that makes the Skills4Peace Framework unique. It takes a seemingly endless list of ideas, recommendations, concepts, rules, principles, directives, and programs about human development, education and behavior and integrates the reasonable and doable ones into an easy-to-understand framework, which if followed will provide a peaceful environment for individuals, families, communities, and societies to exist in harmony together upon this beautiful planet Earth - our home.

VIDEOS FOR EPILOGUE

Childhood Development Initiative (CDI) (2018 May 23) Restorative Practices [Video File]. *YouTube*. Retrieved from https://youtu.be/WyehLeGuLMk

Prevention And Early Intervention Network (2015 April 15) How to implement "The Restorative Practice Programme". [Video File]. *YouTube*. Retrieved from https://youtu.be/1Rm5wqqkPRo

Childhood Development Initiative (CDI) (2014 April 30) restorative practice promo video [Video File]. *YouTube*. Retrieved from https://youtu.be/AfQjYGK5IEU

Childhood Development Initiative (CDI) (2014 April 17) CDI: Restorative Practices Programme [Video File]. *YouTube*. Retrieved from https://youtu.be/ElhsR2519_c

Childhood Development Initiative (CDI) (2015 August 11) Restorative Problem Solving Circle in School [Video File]. *YouTube*. Retrieved from https://youtu.be/vucxpu0_zoI

Childhood Development Initiative (CDI) (2015 August 11) Fishbowl Problem Solving Circle [Video File]. *YouTube*. Retrieved from https://youtu.be/9_5q8zG3o5c

IIRP Graduate School (2010 October 21) Restorative Practices in Hull: The First Restorative City (Trailer) [Video File]. *YouTube*. Retrieved from https://youtu.be/6Qc6zYvnvac

FOOTNOTES
EPILOGUE

1. Simon Corbell, Attorney General, opening speech at the Canberra Restorative Community conference, 7/20/2015
2*https://restorativejustice.org.uk/sites/default/files/resources/files/Towards%20a%20restorative%20city,%20county,%20authority%20or%20community%20-%20Mark%20Finnis_0.pdf*
3. Childhood Development Initiative (2014) A Community-wide Restorative Practices Programme: Implementation Guide. Dublin: Childhood Development Initiative (CDI). https://www.twcdi.ie/wp-content/uploads/2016/11/RP_Implementation_Guide_.pdf
4. Prevention And Early Intervention Network (2015 April 15) How to implement "The Restorative Practice Programme". [Video File].*YouTube.* Retrieved from https://youtu.be/1Rm5wqqkPRo
5. Fives, A., Keenaghan, C., Canavan, J., Moran, L. and Coen, L. (2013) Evaluation of the Restorative Practice Programme of the Childhood Development Initiative. Dublin: Childhood Development Initiative (CDI).

REFERENCES & RESOURCES

RECOMMENDED PROGRAMS
A) PRE – KINDERGARDEN:

"Cool School: Where Peace Rules"

(http://www.coolschoolgame.com) is a free online computer game for parents to play with their preschoolers at:"Cool School" is an interactive computer game designed to teach children about conflict resolution in a lively, fun, entertaining, and developmentally appropriate context. It was developed by interactive gaming veteran F.J. Lennon, whose credits in the industry include projects for the Walt Disney Company, Sesame Street, and Mattel. This game provides children with a positive alternative to the violent images that pervade the video game world. In contrast, this game teaches social skills, and allows children to learn about foundational social skills in a constructive, socially positive, school environment.

The Little Friends for Peace Program (http://www.lffp.org/)was co-founded by MJ and Jerry Park in 1981. "The goal of every LFFP activity is to build Dr. Martin Luther King's Jr's "Beloved Community". Other progressive educators call this work Social and Emotional Learning. MJ and Jerry Park call it educating hearts and minds . . . the Parks provide day camps, in-school and after-school groups and classes, workshops. play shops, retreats, service opportunities and ongoing training, mentoring, and staff development in diverse setting across the U.S and beyond."

Editor's Note from "Live Peace. Teach Peace, Best Practices & Tools" by Mary Joan and Jerry Park.www.LFFP.org

B) K-12: ELEMENTARY & SECONDARY:

ELEMENTARY: *THE FRIENDS SCHOOL OF ST. PAUL MINN.*
The Friends School shares its experience with conflict resolution with other schools by offering:

1) **A training DVD** called *I-to-I: Integrating Conflict Resolution into the Elementary School Community*, an award-winning 35-minute DVD showing the successful conflict resolution program developed and used by Friends School of Minnesota since 1988; and

2) **A training manual**, the product of eight years' use of the program; and

3) **In-person training** in the FSM Conflict Resolution Program for half or full day sessions; 4) **consulting** with principals, teachers, social workers, parents, and other staff. For more information on training & consulting phone: **651-917-0636** (https://fsmn.org/about/our-approach/conflict-resolution):

THE PEACEMAKER PROGRAM AT EDINA, MINN
Johnson, D. W., and R. Johnson. (1991). *Teaching Students to Be Peacemakers*. Edina, Minn.: Interaction Book Company.

THE PEACE CENTER OF BUCKS COUNTY, PA.:
http://www.thepeacecenter.org/programs/project-peace-forschools

THE PEACE FOUNDATION OF NEW ZEALAND:
http: www.peacefoundation.org.nz

C) RESTORATIVE DISCIPLINARY SYSTEMS:

Amstutz, L.S. & Mullet, J.H. (2005) The Little Book of Restorative Discipline for Schools. Intercourse, PA: Good Books

Mara Schiff TED Presentation on Restorative Justice Retrieved from https://www.youtube.com/watch?feature=player_embedded&v=Q4B89j3MrEA

Chicago Video: https://restorativeworks.net/2014/10/chicago-fights-school-prison-pipeline- restoratively

Oakland Video: https://www.youtube.com/watch?v=ZtdoWo1D3sY&feature=player embedded

Philadelphia Video: https://www.youtube.com/watch?v=HatSl1luPM&feature=player embedded

8 Tips for Schools Interested in Restorative Justice | Edutopia
https://www.edutopia.org/blog/restorative-justice-tips-for-schools-fania-davis

D) ADULT EDUCATION FOR ADULTS:

The CRN Online CR Course: http://www.crnhq.org

Successful Negotiation Online Univ. of Michigan course: https://www.coursera.org/learn/negotiation-skills

A mediation course at: freemediationcourse.com

A 40 HR Workplace Mediation Course: mediationworks.com

BIBLIOGRAPHY

Amstutz, Lorraine, The Little Book of Restorative Discipline For Schools. Little Books of Justice & Peacebuilding

Boyes-Watson, C. (2008), Peacemaking circles & Urban Youth, St. Paul: Living Just

Bush, R.A. & Folger, J.P. (2004). *The Promise of Mediation: The Transformative Approach to Conflict.* NY Jossey-Bass, Inc.

Cornelius, H (1998) *The Gentle Revolution.* Sidney: Simon & Schuster

Cornelius, H. & Faire, S. (2006) *Everyone Can Win: responding to conflict constructively.* 2nd edition. Sidney: Simon & Schuster

Costello & Watchel (2013) Restorative Circles in Schools Building Community and Enhancing Learning

Fisher, R. and Ury, W. (1981) *Getting to Yes.* Boston: Houghton Mifflin.

Greenland, Susan Kaiser (2016) Mindful Games. Boulder CO: Shambhala Publishers, Inc.

Harris, Thomas A. (1973) I'm *OK, You're OK*. New York: Avon

Jenner, J.M. and Lederach, J.P. (2002) A Handbook of International Peacebuilding: Into the Eye of the Storm. San Francisco, CA: Jossey-Bass.

Johnson, D. W., and R. Johnson. (1991). *Teaching Students To Be Peacemakers*. Edina, Minn.: Interaction Book Company.

Johnson, K (2013) Unbroken Circles For Schools Tallahassee: Southern Yellow Pine (SYP)Publishing.

Lampken, John (2005) The Peace Kit: Everyday peacemaking for young people. London: Quaker Books

May, Vucki and Rodberg, C.V. (2014) Medicine Wheel Ceremonies. Happy Camp, CA: Naturegraph Publichers, Inc.

Moore, C. (1986). *Mediation*. San Francisco: Jossey-Bass.

O'Connell, T., Wachtel, B. and Wachtel, T. (1999), Conferencing Handbook: The New Real Justice Training Manual, Pipersville, PA: The Piper's Press.

Pavlich, G. (2007), Governing Paradoxes of Restorative Justice, New York: Routledge-Cavendish.

Pranis K. (2005), The little book of circle processes A New/Old Approach to Peacemaking, Intercourse: Good books. Little Books of Justice & Peacebuilding.

Pranis K., Barry S. and Wedge M. (2003), Peacemaking circles: From crime to community, St. Paul: Living Justice Press.

Sunbear, Wind W, and Mulligan C. (1991) Dancing With The Wheel, New York, New York: Fireside Simon & Shuster.

Zehr, Howard (2005) The Little Book of Restorative Justice. Little Books of Justice & Peacebuiding.

READINGS

Belknap, J. and McDonald, C. (2010), 'Judges' Attitudes about and Experiences with Sentencing Circles in Intimate-Partner Abuse Cases', Canadian Journal of Criminology and Criminal Justice, Vol. 52, No. 4.

Bazemore, G. and Umbreit, M. (2001), 'A Comparison of Four Restorative Conferencing Models', Office of Juvenile Justice and Delinquency Prevention Bulletin, February 2001: 1-20.

Boyes-Watson, C. (2005), 'Seeds of change: using peacemaking circles to build a village for every child', Child Welfare, Vol. 84(2):191-208.

Brummer, J., (2020), Building a Trauma-informed Restorative School with Thorsborne, Margaret (2020), Skills and approaches for improving culture and behavior. Kingsley, Jessica Publishers. London (Aus).

Ehret, B. (2012), 'Peacemaking Circles - A Restorative Justice Approach to Extrajudicial Conflict Resolution', Presentation held in Leuven on the 6th December 2012.

Fellegi, Barbara and Szego, Dóra (2010) Handbook for Facilitating Peacemaking Circles in the framework of the project entitled 'Peacemaking Circles in Europe', No. JUST/2010/JPEN/AG/European Commission, DG Justice, Freedom and Security.

Fitzgerald, J. (2008), 'Does circle sentencing reduce Aboriginal offending', Crime and Justice Bulletin, Number115.

Restorative Justice Public Documents (PDFs) retrieved from https://www.nacrj.org/index.php?Itemid=150&option=com_content&view=article&id=16

Greene, R.W., (2016), Raising Human Beings: Creating a Collaborative Partnership with Your Child. Scribner, New York.

Oxendine, Jamie (2014) Native American Medicine Wheel: Comparison In Life –Retrieved from blog: http:// www.powwows.com/native-american-medicine-wheel-comparison-in-life/

Pranis, K., Circle Keeper's Handbook, Retrieved from: http://fromdiaperstodiamonds.com/wp-content/uploads/2015/09/CIRCLE-KEEPER-HANDBOOK-REVISED-PRANIS.pdf

Umbreit, M., Coates, R. and Vos, B. (2007), Restorative justice dialogue: A multiDimensional, Evidence-Based Practice Theory, Contemporary Justice Review, Vol. 10, No. 1: 23-41.

GRAPHICS

WeDoPeace Chart   225

S4P Framework Logo   227

S4P Framework Chart   229

Talking Circle Poster   231

WeDoPeace Circles   233

Know Your Skills4Peace   235

Getting To Peace   237

Skills4Peace Express   239

WE DO PEACE CHART

CONFLICT RESOLUTION

W - When Bullied or Stressed Take a Breath

E - Elect to Respond, Not React

D - Deliver "I" Statements

O - Opt In For a Win/Win

P - Put On & Walk In Their Shoes

E - Engage Willingly In Workout

A - Admit Your Needs & Fears

C - Create Options Together

E - Enter & Do Peace Agreement

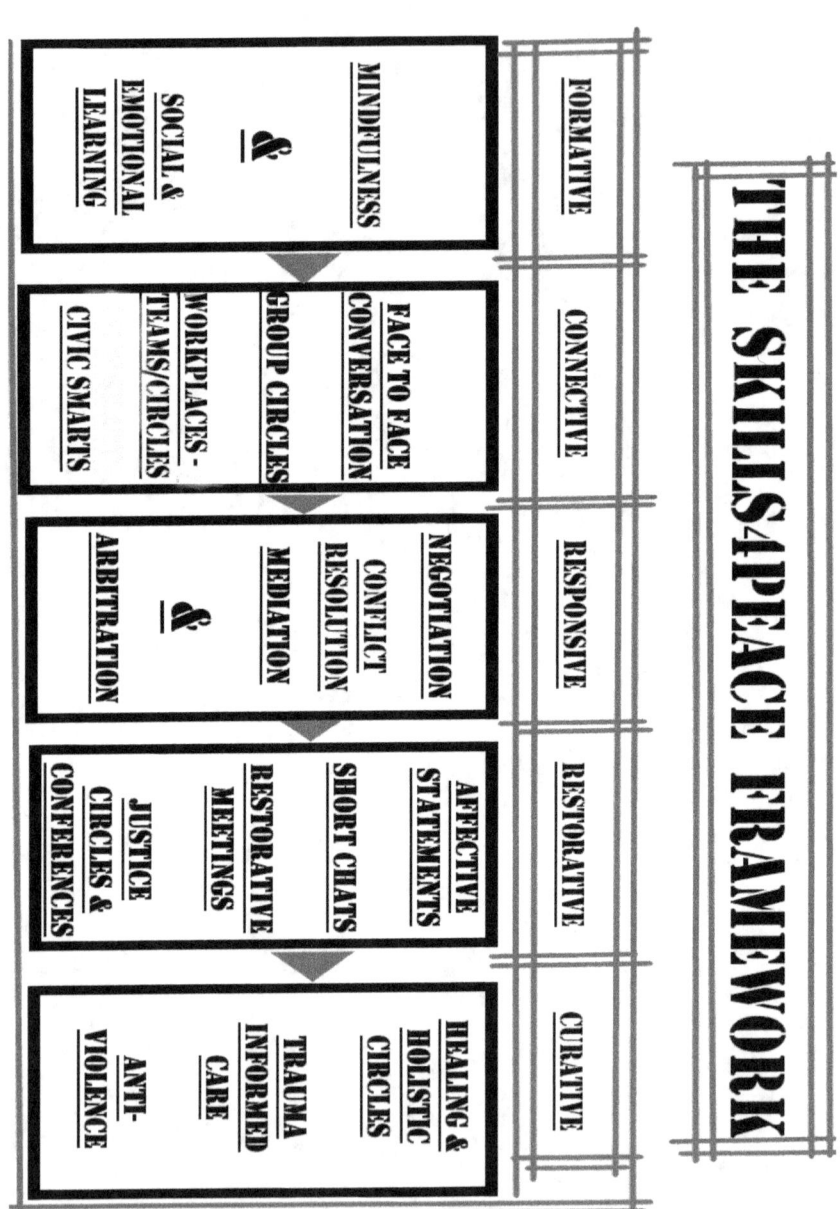

Skills4Peace Framework Chart

I FORMATIVE PEACE SKILLS:
A) Mindfulness: is being intensely aware of what you're sensing and feeling moment to moment without judgment.
B) Social & Emotional Learning (SEL):
Five cognitive, affective & behavioral competencies which are: Self-Awareness, Self-Management, Social Awareness, Relationship Skills and Responsible Decision Making.

II CONNECTIVE PEACE SKILLS
A) Face-To-Face Civil Conversations combine Respectful Speaking & Active Listening by all the parties to a conversation.
B) Group Talking-Piece Circles are meetings in any venue whose participants all use a talking piece to express themselves, build trust, connections & in time a community. (80% of the time).
C) Workplace Teams creating successful collaborative projects using Workplace Conferencing to resolve any problems that may arise.
D) Civic Smarts is a citizen's four-part skill set comprised of Civic Education, Civic Skills, Civic Dispositions, and Action Civics.

III RESPONSIVE PEACE SKILLS:
A) Negotiation - Discussing something with another to reach agreement.
B) Conflict Resolution – Resolving conflict using WEDOPEACE.
C) Mediation - Both sides retain a neutral mediator to assist them.
D) Arbitration – Like litigation it uses a contested trial before a decider.

IV RESTORATIVE PEACE SKILLS:

A) Affective or "I" Statements	(Informal)
B) Affective or Restorative Questions	(Informal)
C) Short & Quick Restorative "Chats"	(Informal)
D) Restorative Meetings (20% of Talking-Piece Circles)	(Semi-formal)
E) Restorative Justice Circles	(Formal)
F) Restorative Conference	(Formal)
G) Family Group Conference	(Formal)

V CURATIVE PEACE SKILLS:
A) Medicine Wheel B) Healing Circles C) Holistic Circles D) Primary Care Circles E) Trauma Induced Care D) CURE – An Anti-Violence Program.

What: <u>A Talking-Piece Circle</u>

Where: _____

When: _____

"We're Saving a Place For You In The Circle"

WeDoPeace Circles
"So We Can All Get Along"

*To Read & Write
Know Your
ABC's ...*

*To Do Peace
Know Your
Skills4Peace!*

*To Get2Peace
Use Your
Skills4Peace!*

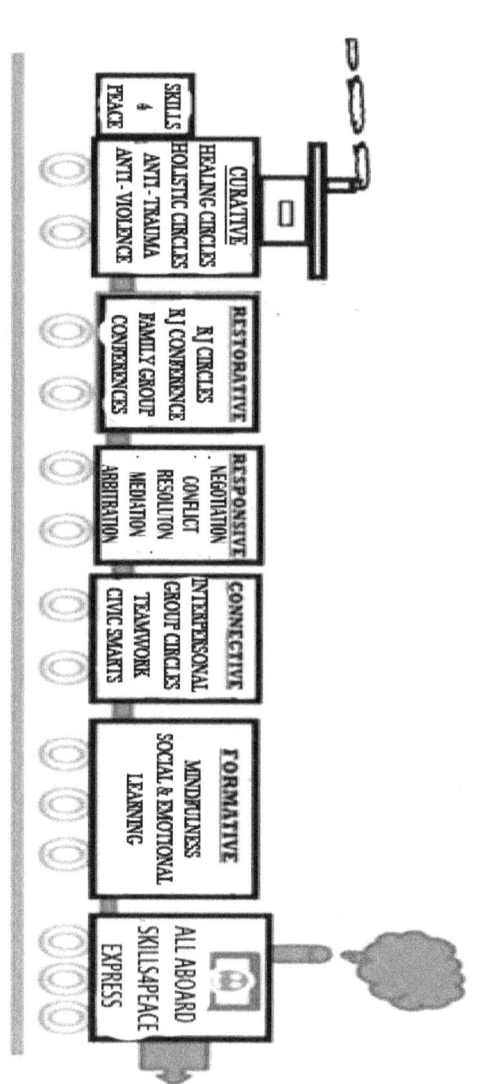

"ALL ABOARD THE SKILLS4PEACE EXPRESS"

APPENDIX

The Constitution of the United States of America is the oldest written constitution still in effect and besides being the fundamental document upon which the government of the United States is based it has also been the model for many other constitutions that have been adopted by countries around the world.

Note: The following text is a transcription of the Constitution as it was inscribed by Jacob Shallus on parchment (the document on display in the Rotunda at the National Archives Museum.)

The spelling and punctuation reflect the original.

A pdf summary of the constitution can be found at: https://www.pbs.org/newshour/classroom/app/uploads/2013/11/summary-of-the-US-Constitution.pdf)

We the People of the United States, in Order to form a more perfect Union, establish Justice, insure domestic Tranquility, provide for the common defence, promote the general Welfare, and secure the Blessings of Liberty to ourselves and our Posterity, do ordain and establish this Constitution for the United States of America.

The Article. I.

Section. 1.

All legislative Powers herein granted shall be vested in a Congress of the United States, which shall consist of a Senate and House of Representatives.

Section. 2.

The House of Representatives shall be composed of Members chosen every second Year by the People of the several States, and the Electors in each State shall have the Qualifications requisite for Electors of the most numerous Branch of the State Legislature.

No Person shall be a Representative who shall not have attained to the Age of twenty five Years, and been seven Years a Citizen of the United States, and who shall not, when elected, be an Inhabitant of that State in which he shall be chosen.

<u>Representatives and direct Taxes shall be apportioned among the several States which may be included within this Union, according to their respective Numbers, which shall be determined by adding to the whole Number of free Persons, including those bound to Service for a Term of Years, and excluding Indians not taxed, three fifths of all other Persons.</u> The actual Enumeration shall be made within three Years after the first Meeting of the Congress of the United States, and within every subsequent Term of ten Years, in such

Manner as they shall by Law direct. The Number of Representatives shall not exceed one for every thirty Thousand, but each State shall have at Least one Representative; and until such enumeration shall be made, the State of New Hampshire shall be entitled to chuse three, Massachusetts eight, Rhode-Island and Providence Plantations one, Connecticut five, New-York six, New Jersey four, Pennsylvania eight, Delaware one, Maryland six, Virginia ten, North Carolina five, South Carolina five, and Georgia three.

When vacancies happen in the Representation from any State, the Executive Authority thereof shall issue Writs of Election to fill such Vacancies.

The House of Representatives shall chuse their Speaker and other Officers; and shall have the sole Power of Impeachment.

Section. 3.

The Senate of the United States shall be composed of two Senators from each State, <u>chosen by the Legislature</u> thereof, for six Years; and each Senator shall have one Vote.

Immediately after they shall be assembled in Consequence of the first Election, they shall be divided as equally as may be into three Classes. The Seats of the Senators of the first Class shall be vacated at the Expiration of the second Year, of the second Class at the Expiration of the fourth Year, and of the third Class at the Expiration of the sixth Year, so that one third may be chosen every second Year; <u>and if Vacancies happen by Resignation, or otherwise, during the Recess of the Legislature of any State, the Executive thereof may make temporary Appointments until the next Meeting of the Legislature, which shall then fill such Vacancies.</u>

No Person shall be a Senator who shall not have attained to the Age of thirty Years, and been nine Years a Citizen of the United States, and who shall not, when elected, be an Inhabitant of that State for which he shall be chosen.

The Vice President of the United States shall be President of the Senate, but shall have no Vote, unless they be equally divided.

The Senate shall chuse their other Officers, and also a President pro tempore, in the Absence of the Vice President, or when he shall exercise the Office of President of the United States.

The Senate shall have the sole Power to try all Impeachments. When sitting for that Purpose, they shall be on Oath or Affirmation. When the President of the United States is tried, the Chief Justice shall preside: And no Person shall be convicted without the Concurrence of two thirds of the Members present.

Judgment in Cases of Impeachment shall not extend further than to removal from Office, and disqualification to hold and enjoy any Office of honor, Trust or Profit under the United States: but the Party convicted shall nevertheless be liable and subject to Indictment, Trial, Judgment and Punishment, according to Law.

Section. 4.

The Times, Places and Manner of holding Elections for Senators and Representatives, shall be prescribed in each State by the Legislature thereof; but the Congress may at any time by Law make or alter such Regulations, except as to the Places of chusing Senators.

The Congress shall assemble at least once in every Year, and such Meeting shall be on <u>the first Monday in December</u>, unless they shall by Law appoint a different Day.

Section. 5.

Each House shall be the Judge of the Elections, Returns and Qualifications of its own Members, and a Majority of each shall constitute a Quorum to do Business; but a smaller Number may adjourn from day to day, and may be authorized to compel the Attendance of absent Members, in such Manner, and under such Penalties as each House may provide.

Each House may determine the Rules of its Proceedings, punish its Members for disorderly Behaviour, and, with the Concurrence of two thirds, expel a Member.

Each House shall keep a Journal of its Proceedings, and from time to time publish the same, excepting such Parts as may in their Judgment require Secrecy; and the

Yeas and Nays of the Members of either House on any question shall, at the Desire of one fifth of those Present, be entered on the Journal.

Neither House, during the Session of Congress, shall, without the Consent of the other, adjourn for more than three days, nor to any other Place than that in which the two Houses shall be sitting.

Section. 6.

The Senators and Representatives shall receive a Compensation for their Services, to be ascertained by Law, and paid out of the Treasury of the United States. They shall in all Cases, except Treason, Felony and Breach of the Peace, be privileged from Arrest during their Attendance at the Session of their respective Houses, and in going to and returning from the same; and for any Speech or Debate in either House, they shall not be questioned in any other Place.

No Senator or Representative shall, during the Time for which he was elected, be appointed to any civil Office under the Authority of the United States, which shall have been created, or the Emoluments whereof shall have been encreased during such time; and no Person holding any Office under the United States, shall be a Member of either House during his Continuance in Office.

Section. 7.

All Bills for raising Revenue shall originate in the House of Representatives; but the Senate may propose or concur with Amendments as on other Bills.

Every Bill which shall have passed the House of Representatives and the Senate, shall, before it become a Law, be presented to the President of the United States; If he approve he shall sign it, but if not he shall return it, with his Objections to that House in which it shall have originated, who shall enter the Objections at large on their Journal, and proceed to reconsider it. If after such Reconsideration two thirds of that House shall agree to pass the Bill, it shall be sent, together with the Objections, to the other House, by which it shall likewise be reconsidered, and if approved by two thirds of that House, it shall become a Law. But in all such Cases the Votes of both Houses shall be determined by yeas and Nays, and the Names of the Persons voting for and against the Bill shall be entered on the Journal of each House respectively. If any Bill shall not be returned by the President within ten Days (Sundays excepted) after it shall have been presented to him, the Same shall be a Law, in like Manner as if he had signed it, unless the Congress by their Adjournment prevent its Return, in which Case it shall not be a Law.

Every Order, Resolution, or Vote to which the Concurrence of the Senate and House of Representatives may be necessary (except on a question of Adjournment) shall be presented to the

President of the United States; and before the Same shall take Effect, shall be approved by him, or being disapproved by him, shall be repassed by two thirds of the Senate and House of Representatives, according to the Rules and Limitations prescribed in the Case of a Bill.

Section. 8.

The Congress shall have Power To lay and collect Taxes, Duties, Imposts and Excises, to pay the Debts and provide for the common Defence and general Welfare of the United States; but all Duties, Imposts and Excises shall be uniform throughout the United States;

To borrow Money on the credit of the United States;

To regulate Commerce with foreign Nations, and among the several States, and with the Indian Tribes;

To establish an uniform Rule of Naturalization, and uniform Laws on the subject of Bankruptcies throughout the United States;

To coin Money, regulate the Value thereof, and of foreign Coin, and fix the Standard of Weights and Measures;

To provide for the Punishment of counterfeiting the Securities and current Coin of the United States;

To establish Post Offices and post Roads;

To promote the Progress of Science and useful Arts, by securing for limited Times to Authors and Inventors the exclusive Right to their respective Writings and Discoveries;

To constitute Tribunals inferior to the supreme Court;

To define and punish Piracies and Felonies committed on the high Seas, and Offences against the Law of Nations;

To declare War, grant Letters of Marque and Reprisal, and make Rules concerning Captures on Land and Water;

To raise and support Armies, but no Appropriation of Money to that Use shall be for a longer Term than two Years;

To provide and maintain a Navy;

To make Rules for the Government and Regulation of the land and naval Forces;

To provide for calling forth the Militia to execute the Laws of the Union, suppress Insurrections and repel Invasions;

To provide for organizing, arming, and disciplining, the Militia, and for governing such Part of them as may be employed in the Service of the United States, reserving to the States respectively, the Appointment of the Officers, and the Authority of training the Militia according to the discipline prescribed by Congress;

To exercise exclusive Legislation in all Cases whatsoever, over such District (not exceeding ten Miles square) as may, by Cession of particular States, and the Acceptance of Congress, become the Seat of the Government of the United States, and to exercise like Authority over all Places purchased by the Consent of the Legislature of the State in which the Same shall be, for the Erection of Forts, Magazines, Arsenals, dock-Yards, and other needful Buildings;—And

To make all Laws which shall be necessary and proper for carrying into Execution the foregoing Powers, and all other Powers vested by this Constitution in the Government of the United States, or in any Department or Officer thereof.

Section. 9.

The Migration or Importation of such Persons as any of the States now existing shall think proper to admit, shall not be prohibited by the Congress prior to the Year one thousand eight hundred and eight, but a Tax or duty may be imposed on such Importation, not exceeding ten dollars for each Person.

The Privilege of the Writ of Habeas Corpus shall not be suspended, unless when in Cases of Rebellion or Invasion the public Safety may require it.

No Bill of Attainder or ex post facto Law shall be passed.

No Capitation, or other direct, Tax shall be laid, <u>unless in Proportion to the Census or enumeration herein before directed to be taken.</u>

No Tax or Duty shall be laid on Articles exported from any State.

No Preference shall be given by any Regulation of Commerce or Revenue to the Ports of one State over those of another: nor shall Vessels bound to, or from, one State, be obliged to enter, clear, or pay Duties in another.

No Money shall be drawn from the Treasury, but in Consequence of Appropriations made by Law; and a regular Statement and Account of the Receipts and Expenditures of all public Money shall be published from time to time.

No Title of Nobility shall be granted by the United States: And no Person holding any Office of Profit or Trust under them, shall, without the Consent of the Congress, accept of any present, Emolument, Office, or Title, of any kind whatever, from any King, Prince, or foreign State.

Section. 10.

No State shall enter into any Treaty, Alliance, or Confederation; grant Letters of Marque and Reprisal; coin Money; emit Bills of Credit; make any Thing but gold and silver Coin a Tender in Payment of Debts; pass any Bill of Attainder, ex post facto Law, or Law impairing the Obligation of Contracts, or grant any Title of Nobility.

No State shall, without the Consent of the Congress, lay any Imposts or Duties on Imports or Exports, except what may be absolutely necessary for executing it's inspection Laws: and the net Produce of all Duties and Imposts, laid by any State on Imports or Exports, shall be for the Use of the Treasury of the United States; and all such Laws shall be subject to the Revision and Controul of the Congress.

No State shall, without the Consent of Congress, lay any Duty of Tonnage, keep Troops, or Ships of War in time of Peace, enter into any Agreement or Compact with another State, or with a foreign Power, or engage in War, unless actually invaded, or in such imminent Danger as will not admit of delay.

Article. II.

Section. 1.

The executive Power shall be vested in a President of the United States of America. He shall hold his Office during the Term of four Years, and, together with the Vice President, chosen for the same Term, be elected, as follows

Each State shall appoint, in such Manner as the Legislature thereof may direct, a Number of Electors, equal to the whole Number of Senators and Representatives to which the State may be entitled in the Congress: but no Senator or Representative, or Person holding an Office of Trust or Profit under the United States, shall be appointed an Elector.

The Electors shall meet in their respective States, and vote by Ballot for two Persons, of whom one at least shall not be an Inhabitant of the same State with themselves. And they shall make a List of all the Persons voted for, and of the Number of Votes for each; which List they shall sign and certify, and transmit sealed to the Seat of the Government of the United States, directed to the President of the Senate. The President of the Senate shall, in the Presence of the Senate and House of Representatives, open all the Certificates, and the Votes shall then be counted. The Person having the greatest Number of Votes shall be the President, if such Number be a Majority of the whole Number of Electors appointed; and if there be more than one who have such Majority, and have an equal Number of Votes, then the House of Representatives shall immediately chuse by Ballot one of them for President; and if no Person have a Majority, then from the five highest on the List the said House shall in like Manner chuse the President. But in chusing the President, the Votes shall be taken by States, the Representation from each State having one Vote; A quorum for this Purpose shall consist of a Member or Members from two thirds of the States, and a Majority of all the States shall be necessary to a Choice. In every Case, after the Choice of the President, the Person having the greatest Number of Votes of the Electors shall be the Vice President. But if there should remain two or more who have equal Votes, the Senate shall chuse from them by Ballot the Vice President.

The Congress may determine the Time of chusing the Electors, and the Day on which they shall give their Votes; which Day shall be the same throughout the United States.

No Person except a natural born Citizen, or a Citizen of the United States, at the time of the Adoption of this Constitution, shall be eligible to the Office of President; neither shall any Person be eligible to that Office who shall not have attained to the Age of thirty five Years, and been fourteen Years a Resident within the United States.

In Case of the Removal of the President from Office, or of his Death, Resignation, or Inability to discharge the Powers and Duties of the said Office, the Same shall devolve on the Vice President, and the Congress may by Law provide for the Case of Removal, Death, Resignation or Inability, both of the President and Vice President, declaring what Officer shall then act as President, and such Officer shall act accordingly, until the Disability be removed, or a President shall be elected.

The President shall, at stated Times, receive for his Services, a Compensation, which shall neither be encreased nor diminished during the Period for which he shall have been elected, and he shall not receive within that Period any other Emolument from the United States, or any of them.

Before he enter on the Execution of his Office, he shall take the following Oath or Affirmation:—"I do solemnly swear (or affirm) that I will faithfully execute the Office of President of the United States, and will to the best of my Ability, preserve, protect and defend the Constitution of the United States."

Section. 2.

The President shall be Commander in Chief of the Army and Navy of the United States, and of the Militia of the several States, when called into the actual Service of the United States; he may require the Opinion, in writing, of the principal Officer in each of the executive Departments, upon any Subject relating to the Duties of their respective Offices, and he shall have Power to grant Reprieves and Pardons for Offences against the United States, except in Cases of Impeachment.

He shall have Power, by and with the Advice and Consent of the Senate, to make Treaties, provided two thirds of the Senators present concur; and he shall nominate, and by and with the Advice and Consent of the Senate, shall appoint Ambassadors, other public Ministers and Consuls, Judges of the supreme Court, and all other Officers of the United States, whose Appointments are not herein otherwise provided for, and which shall be established by Law: but the Congress may by Law vest the Appointment of such inferior

Officers, as they think proper, in the President alone, in the Courts of Law, or in the Heads of Departments.

The President shall have Power to fill up all Vacancies that may happen during the Recess of the Senate, by granting Commissions which shall expire at the End of their next Session.

Section. 3.

He shall from time to time give to the Congress Information of the State of the Union, and recommend to their Consideration such Measures as he shall judge necessary and expedient; he may, on extraordinary Occasions, convene both Houses, or either of them, and in Case of Disagreement between them, with Respect to the Time of Adjournment, he may adjourn them to such Time as he shall think proper; he shall receive Ambassadors and other public Ministers; he shall take Care that the Laws be faithfully executed, and shall Commission all the Officers of the United States.

Section. 4.

The President, Vice President and all civil Officers of the United States, shall be removed from Office on Impeachment for, and Conviction of, Treason, Bribery, or other high Crimes and Misdemeanors.

Article III.

Section. 1.

The judicial Power of the United States shall be vested in one supreme Court, and in such inferior Courts as the Congress may from time to time ordain and establish. The Judges, both of the supreme and inferior Courts, shall hold their Offices during good Behaviour, and shall, at stated Times, receive for their Services, a Compensation, which shall not be diminished during their Continuance in Office.

Section. 2.

The judicial Power shall extend to all Cases, in Law and Equity, arising under this Constitution, the Laws of the United States, and Treaties made, or which shall be made, under their Authority;—to all Cases affecting Ambassadors, other public Ministers and Consuls;—to all Cases of admiralty and maritime Jurisdiction;—to Controversies to which the United States shall be a Party;—to Controversies between two or more States;— <u>between a State and Citizens of another State</u>,—between Citizens of different States,—between Citizens of the same State claiming Lands under Grants of different States, and between a State, or the Citizens thereof, and foreign States, Citizens or Subjects.

In all Cases affecting Ambassadors, other public Ministers and Consuls, and those in which a State shall be Party, the supreme Court shall have original Jurisdiction. In all the other Cases before mentioned, the supreme Court shall have appellate Jurisdiction, both as to Law and Fact, with such Exceptions, and under such Regulations as the Congress shall make.

The Trial of all Crimes, except in Cases of Impeachment, shall be by Jury; and such Trial shall be held in the State where the said Crimes shall have been committed; but when not committed within any State, the Trial shall be at such Place or Places as the Congress may by Law have directed.

Section. 3.

Treason against the United States, shall consist only in levying War against them, or in adhering to their Enemies, giving them Aid and Comfort. No Person shall be convicted of Treason unless on the Testimony of two Witnesses to the same overt Act, or on Confession in open Court.

The Congress shall have Power to declare the Punishment of Treason, but no Attainder of Treason shall work Corruption of Blood, or Forfeiture except during the Life of the Person attainted.

Article. IV.

Section. 1.

Full Faith and Credit shall be given in each State to the public Acts, Records, and judicial Proceedings of every other State. And the Congress may by general Laws prescribe the Manner in which such Acts, Records and Proceedings shall be proved, and the Effect thereof.

Section. 2.

The Citizens of each State shall be entitled to all Privileges and Immunities of Citizens in the several States.

A Person charged in any State with Treason, Felony, or other Crime, who shall flee from Justice, and be found in another State, shall on Demand of the executive Authority of the State from which he fled, be delivered up, to be removed to the State having Jurisdiction of the Crime.

<u>No Person held to Service or Labour in one State, under the Laws thereof, escaping into another, shall, in Consequence of any Law or Regulation therein, be discharged from such Service or Labour, but shall be delivered up on Claim of the Party to whom such Service or Labour may be due.</u>

Section. 3.

New States may be admitted by the Congress into this Union; but no new State shall be formed or erected within the Jurisdiction of any other State; nor any State be formed by the Junction of two or more States, or Parts of States, without the Consent of the Legislatures of the States concerned as well as of the Congress.

The Congress shall have Power to dispose of and make all needful Rules and Regulations respecting the Territory or other Property belonging to the United States; and nothing in this Constitution shall be so construed as to Prejudice any Claims of the United States, or of any particular State.

Section. 4.

The United States shall guarantee to every State in this Union a Republican Form of Government, and shall protect each of them against Invasion; and on Application of the Legislature, or of the Executive (when the Legislature cannot be convened) against domestic Violence.

Article. V.

The Congress, whenever two thirds of both Houses shall deem it necessary, shall propose Amendments to this Constitution, or, on the Application of the Legislatures of two thirds of the several States, shall call a Convention for proposing Amendments, which, in either Case, shall be valid to all Intents and Purposes, as Part of this Constitution, when ratified by the Legislatures of three fourths of the several States, or by Conventions in three fourths thereof, as the one or the other Mode of Ratification may be proposed by the Congress; Provided that no Amendment which may be made prior to the Year One thousand eight hundred and eight shall in any Manner affect the first and fourth Clauses in the Ninth Section of the first Article; and that no State, without its Consent, shall be deprived of its equal Suffrage in the Senate.

Article. VI.

All Debts contracted and Engagements entered into, before the Adoption of this Constitution, shall be as valid against the United States under this Constitution, as under the Confederation.

This Constitution, and the Laws of the United States which shall be made in Pursuance thereof; and all Treaties made, or which shall be made, under the Authority of the United States, shall be the supreme Law of the Land; and the Judges in every State shall be bound thereby, any Thing in the Constitution or Laws of any State to the Contrary notwithstanding.

The Senators and Representatives before mentioned, and the Members of the several State Legislatures, and all executive and judicial Officers, both of the United States and of the several States, shall be bound by Oath or Affirmation, to support this Constitution; but no religious Test shall ever be required as a Qualification to any Office or public Trust under the United States.

Article. VII.

The Ratification of the Conventions of nine States, shall be sufficient for the Establishment of this Constitution between the States so ratifying the Same.

The Word, "the," being interlined between the seventh and eighth Lines of the first Page, The Word "Thirty" being partly written on an Erazure in the fifteenth Line of the first Page, The Words "is tried" being interlined between the thirty second and thirty third Lines of the first Page and the Word "the" being interlined between the forty third and forty fourth Lines of the second Page.

Attest William Jackson Secretary

done in Convention by the Unanimous Consent of the States present the Seventeenth Day of September in the Year of our Lord one thousand seven hundred and Eighty seven and of the Independance of the United States of America the Twelfth In witness whereof We have hereunto subscribed our Names,

G°. Washington
Presidt and deputy from Virginia"

Amendments To the Constitution of the USA

Amendment 1 - Freedom of speech, press, religion, assembly, and petition.

Amendment 2 - Right to bear arms.

Amendment 3 - Citizens do not have to house soldiers.

Amendment 4 - No unreasonable search or arrest.

Amendment 5 - No double jeopardy nor witness against oneself.

Amendment 6 - The right to a speedy and public trial

Amendment 7 - The right to a jury trial in civil matters

Amendment 8 - No excessive bail or cruel punishment.

Amendment 9 - People get rights not listed herein.

Amendment 10 - Any rights not given to federal government are given to the states and people.

Amendment 11- Individual cannot sue a state in a federal court.

Amendment 12 - Separate ballots for Pres and V Pres.

Amendment 13 - Abolish slavery.

Amendment 14 - If you are born or naturalized in the U.S. then you are a citizen of the U.S.

Amendment 15 - You cannot prevent a person from voting because of race, color, or creed.

Amendment 16 - Income tax.

Amendment 17- Popular election of U.S. Senators.

Amendment 18 - Prohibition.

Amendment 19 - Women get the right to vote.

Amendment 20 - President takes office on January 20th instead of March 4th.

Amendment 21- Repeal prohibition.

Amendment 22- President can only serve two terms.

Amendment 23 - D.C. residents can vote for president.

Amendment 24 - Anti poll tax.

Amendment 25 - Lays down the rules for who becomes president if the president dies or resigns.

Amendment 26 - 18-year-olds get the vote.

Amendment 27 - Congress cannot accept a pay raise until next term.